BUILDING
THE RIGHT
THINGS RIGHT

A New Model for Product and Technology Development

Charles J. Nuese

QUALITY RESOURCES®
A Division of The Kraus Organization Limited
New York, New York

Most Quality Resources books are available at quantity discounts when purchased in bulk. For more information contact:

Special Sales Department
Quality Resources
A Division of The Kraus Organization Limited
902 Broadway
New York, New York 10010
800-247-8519

Printed in the United States of America

99 98 97 96 95   10 9 8 7 6 5 4 3 2 1

Quality Resources
A Division of The Kraus
  Organization Limited
902 Broadway
New York, New York 10010
212-979-8600
800-247-8519

This book is also distributed by:

AMACOM Books, a division of
American Management Association
135 West 50th Street
New York, NY 10020

The paper used in this publication meets the minimum requirements of American National Standard for Information Sciences—Permanence of Paper for Printed Library Materials, ANSI Z39.48-1984.

ISBN 0-527-76300-4 (Quality Resources)
ISBN 0-8144-0302-6 (AMACOM Books)

Library of Congress Cataloging-in-Publication Data

Nuese, Charles J.
    Building the right things right : a new model for product and technology
    development / by Charles J. Nuese.
        p.   cm.
    Includes index.
    ISBN 0-527-76300-4, — ISBN 0-8144-0302-6
    1. New products.   2. Production engineering.   3. Concurrent
engineering.   I. Title.
TS170.N83   1995
658.5'75—dc20   95-14651
                                                                    CIP

This book is dedicated to my wife, Dodi, our children, Jeff, Kathi, and Sue, and our grandchildren, Katie and Jackie.

It is done so in memory of my parents and sister.

Contents

List of Figures

List of Tables

Acknowledgments

The completion of any significant activity requires the assistance and support of many contributors—and the preparation of this book is no exception. Many of my personal insights regarding product and technology development have evolved over a 25-year period at four organizations:

At the SRI Sarnoff Research Center, which was then RCA Laboratories, where I was taught the importance of a business perspective in R&D by Len Weisberg, Jim Tietjen, Bob Lohman, and Henry Kressel. From coworkers Mike Ettenberg, Greg Olsen, and Larry Goodman, I learned the value of effective teamwork.

At RCA Solid State, which eventually became GE Semiconductor, where Hesh Khajezadeh, Carl Turner, and Eric Burlefinger showed me the importance of metrics, and how they can be used to drive progress in technology and manufacturing.

And at Harris Semiconductor, where I was fortunate to be a part of the revolution associated with self-directed work teams and the implementation of a formal development process. Here, I wish to thank Jack Corley, Jon Cornell, Dale Edwards, Walt Fredrickson, Miriam Martinez, Russ Morcom, Jeff Peters, Geoff Phillips, Ken Ports, and Gary Tighe for their suggestions and contributions.

This book originated from a study that was supported by the Semiconductor Research Corporation. The encouragement of Bob Burger, Linda Gardner, Larry Sumney, and Jim Freedman of the SRC helped me begin documenting this work. Professors Wade Shaw and Roger Manley of the Florida Institute of Technology also helped me with a study of the university research process, some of which is discussed in Chapter 11.

Many companies have allowed me to use one or more of their graphics in the preparation of this manuscript. For their courtesy, I wish to acknowledge the American Electronics Association, Arthur D. Little Incorporated, Automotive News, Irwin Professional Publishing Company, Business Week Magazine, Dataquest Incorporated, Electronic Business Magazine, Fortune Magazine, Harris Corporation, Hewlett Packard Company, Hughes Aircraft Company, the Industrial Research Institute, the Institute of Defense Analysis, KPMG Peat Marwick, McKinsey and Company, the MIT International Motor Vehicle Program, the National Center for Advanced Technology, the National Center for Manufacturing Sciences, the National Science Foundation, Pittiglio Rabin Todd and McGrath, the Semiconductor Research Corporation, and Strategic Alternatives Incorporated. I'd like to extend a special thanks to Vicor Corporation, Xilinx, Sun Microsystems, and Cadence Design Systems, who were kind enough to supply me with artwork for the product advertisements in Chapter 2.

Thanks also go to John Willig and Associates, my literary agent, and to Hollis Barnhart and Mike Sinocchi of Quality Resources, who helped shape the final form of this work.

And finally, I'd like to acknowledge my greatest appreciation for the support of my family—those who have passed on, and those who continue to brighten each day. Through it all, my wife Dodi stands beside me, bringing a smile to my lips and pride to my heart.

Introduction

A TIME OF CHANGE

By now, the story's been told: how American industry was caught napping through the '60s and '70s—confident that its manufacturing and technology strengths would prevail, and largely indifferent to the embryonic efforts across the sea to put quality into manufacturing and pride into workmanship. After all, the United States gave birth to the Industrial Revolution. We invented and developed most of the tools of modern technology, founded the electronic and computer age, and were understandably pleased with their impact on our lifestyle. Although we were generally aware of the cheap labor market in the Far East, the United States dominated nearly all sectors of world technology, including automobiles, steel, and consumer electronics. Our global concerns were directed primarily to the cold war and competition with the Soviet Union in defense and space technologies.

By the mid-'70s, the Japanese were well on their way to capturing consumer electronics—first, as a high-volume, low-cost manufacturing extension of the United States and soon thereafter with their own product capabilities. These were centered around rapid movements into and out of the market, superior manufacturing quality, and a watchful eye on consumer needs. Since that time, global technology leadership in many technical areas has shifted ever eastward.

The wake-up call arrived in the United States in the early '80s, occurring at slightly different times for different industries and different companies. After nearly 40 years of domination, the United States found itself in a struggle for economic survival. The weapons of battle were products, borne from state-of-the-art technologies from foreign lands. And the casualties were the human victims of economic stagnation, many from such once-great manufacturing cities as Detroit and Pittsburgh. There really were no enemies, just competitors, but that fact provided little comfort to idle factories and down-sized workers.

Gradually an awareness crept in regarding the importance of rapid product development, as new products, developed nearly overnight, hastened the obsolescence of their predecessors and shortened market windows. In the computer industry, a product generation was fortunate to last 18 months. Equally important was the need for matching product capabilities to customer requirements. The indiscriminate addition of technical bells and whistles loaded product costs to the point at which consumers rejected them—in a market rife with choices.

Moreover, the efficiency of the U.S. development process was found lacking—often providing products that were over schedule, over budget, and over priced. We've now come to appreciate:

- Dedicated and empowered work teams—unencumbered by traditional management delays.

- Managers who relinquish control to their workers, so that decisions can be made by those who know the most about the problems.

- Products that are designed with low-cost production in mind.

- Customer partnerships, to ensure that product benefits match market requirements.

In the last few years, some U.S. companies have begun to win their market battles—in fact, more and more are doing so every day. And those that win most often are very different companies than they were 10 years ago. The development process is at the heart of the change. For with today's rapid product obsolescence, the need for early market entry is imperative. Products must also be carefully aligned with customer needs to be successful.

However, there are gross variations across the U.S. business world in the effectiveness of the product development process. Some companies have been at it for nearly a decade, while others are just beginning. But most major companies are involved to some extent in changing the paradigm for new product and technology development—from a series process to a concurrent one; from micromanagers to work teams; from engineering isolation to customer involvement; and most of all, *from slow to fast!*

But the changes are painful because they involve nearly all employees and because they require dramatically different approaches toward engineering and scientific development. This book addresses these changes as they explode across our nation. The product development path has already been traveled by others; but what worked for them, may not for us.

WHAT'S A PRODUCT?

According to the *American-Heritage Dictionary*,[1] a *product* is "something that is produced naturally or by human effort; a direct result." *Production* is "the act or process of producing."

Obviously, the general definition of a product is broad. A tree is a product of nature (i.e., sunshine, oxygen, moisture, etc.). So, therefore, is a salmon or a mountain. In this book, we will focus only on products that are produced, grown, or created intentionally by human efforts. We will

---

[1] *The American Heritage Dictionary* (Dell, 1994), p. 660.

further bound the definition in a business sense as follows: a *business product* is something that is produced through a serious work effort intended to maximize its business impact, while effectively using resources.

Products can be manufactured in factories, grown on a farm, or scribed by pen. They can be hardware, software, butter, or bullets. Complexity is not a factor; products range from table salt to banquet feasts, from poems to encyclopedias, and from paper clips to nuclear power generators. To meet our definition, business products should simply serve a serious business purpose (to have an impact), and should be developed through effective use of resources—including time, cost, materials, labor, and equipment.

Many human efforts do not result in business products. For example, a hobby often produces significant accomplishments (including enjoyment and self-gratification), but usually with little regard for optimizing resources, including time and expenses. A do-it-yourself project also does not produce a product from a business perspective, because there is usually no serious intention of selling the result for monetary gain. Moreover, not many people would be kind enough to use the word *serious* to describe some of my home projects!

The phrase (and title of this book) "building the right things right" describes the two goals of any product that is intended to be developed for successful business impact:

1. The product should serve its intended purpose well, meet the needs of its customers, and fall within the capabilities and charter of the company developing it. That is, it should be *the right product.*

2. It also should be developed with acceptable quality and with an effective use of resources. That is, it *should be built right.*

For example, in the development of a pencil, considerations regarding making the right product might include the intended market segment (souvenir, youth, general public, or professional applications), the type of pencil (mechanical, plain wooden, or thin-lead drafting), distribution channel (wholesale, retail, or mail-order), and market competition. Considerations for making the product right might include the material selection, design style, assembly and packaging equipment, labor costs, scrap losses, and development cycle time.

If the product were an article for commercial publication, defining the right product might include subject selection, the demographics of the intended readers, the candidate magazines, the approximate length, and the prospects for obtaining a publishing commitment. Producing the product right might involve the choice of writing tools, the correctness of the grammar, appeal of the writing style, and the author's availability and productivity in completing the manuscript on schedule.

In these examples, and in just about any other real business efforts, each objective—doing the right product and doing the product right—is equally important for overall success.

THE DEVELOPMENT PROCESS

From the perspective of a worker assigned to a new product, development can be a highly unique experience. The product might have an unusual set of boundary conditions, associates who have not previously worked together, aggressive schedules, limited resources, fierce market competition, and technical specifications that differ dramatically from those of other company products. Yet within a single company, or even a single department, this scenario repeats itself over and over. The experience is individually unique—but collectively repetitive.

> First and foremost, product and technology development is a process.

In this book, we will show that the process is much the same for many different types of products. It begins with a concept and ends with manufacturing and sales support. We do not focus on any single element, such as concurrent engineering, TQM, or continuous improvement, because others have covered these subjects. Instead, "Building the RIGHT Things RIGHT" describes how to put them all together.

With the need for change foremost in our mind, this book provides a recipe for modern product and technology development. It describes a generic five-step process for just about any type of product, one that is extendible to enabling technology and even to applied research. The process guides a development team through the phases of advanced planning and product definition, where the right product is established, followed by design, demonstration, and customer support phases, where the focus is on developing the product right.

"Building the RIGHT Things RIGHT" provides the reader with an assessment of the new product and technology development paradigm in U.S. industry and universities. In the former case, major differences arise between small and large companies. For our technical universities—the source of much of our emerging technology base—the new development paradigm is only beginning to be understood and supported. A university leadership position in this area is still many years away.

In progressing through this book, the reader will discover a style and format that differs from that of most business-oriented volumes. I'm often disappointed with popular business literature that consists primarily of a collection of interesting stories and folklore about a specific business method. In such cases, examples are usually selected to support the author's views, while numeric, quantifiable results are rarely included. In "Building the RIGHT Things RIGHT," I have tried to fill these pages with substance—in the form of quotes, charts, surveys, numerical data, and even advertisement copy taken from current periodicals and business journals to support the topic of discussion. These are complemented with how-to recipes that separate what works from what doesn't.

There will almost certainly be better ways of developing products in the future. But for now, and for the next several years, the paradigm described within is being embraced in our best companies and organizations—the ones that will still be here for years to come.

CHAPTER 1

Time

for a

Change

With a few exceptions, the United States has dominated most of the economic markets since World War II. However, during the 1970s and 1980s, great progress was made by several of our global competitors, most notably Japan and Germany. Today, the United States is still the largest economic force, with greater manufacturing productivity, R&D investment, and broad-based market share than any other country. But our lead is dropping fast. Japan especially has tied its future to high technology and is gaining a world-wide market share in it; South Korea, Singapore, and Taiwan seem to have the same strategy and are following in Japan's footsteps. Some markets have completely fallen from our grasp—for example, consumer electronics. After a decade of losing ground, the automotive market is now pretty much a dead heat between the United States and Japan. We're in the thick of it with steel, lumber, and textiles, and that's encouraging, but we used to own these markets.

Clearly, across many industries and technologies, our once-dominant position has eroded. In particular, consider the following:

- Over the past 30 years, the United States has ranked lower than nearly all industrial countries in the rate of productivity growth. Over most of this time, the productivity of U.S. workers has increased by only a fraction of a percent a year—far less than that of other countries (see Figure 1.1). Between 1975 and 1991, South Korea has increased its worker productivity by 5 percent per year![1]

- The United States has the lowest rate of capital investment of any major industrial country.[2] At 4.7 percent, it also has the lowest personal savings rate.[3]

- Service now accounts for more than half of the U.S. gross domestic product.[4]

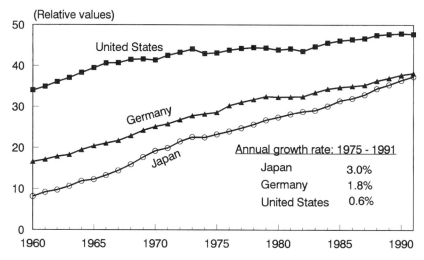

FIGURE 1.1. Gross domestic product for the United States, Germany, and Japan.
SOURCE: *Science and Engineering Indicators—1993*, p. 439.

---

[1]*Science and Engineering Indicators—1993* (National Science Board, U.S. Government Printing Office, 1993), p. 437.

[2]J. P. Grace, "Removing the False Assumptions from Economic Policy Making," *Productivity—A National Priority* (Pepperdine University Press, Malibu, CA, 1982), p. 9.

[3]*The American Almanac 1993–1994: Statistical Abstract of the United States* (Reference Press, Inc., Austin, TX, 1993), p. 445. *Focus* (National Center for Manufacturing Sciences, Ann Arbor, MI), p. 2, June 1992.

[4]*The American Almanac 1993–1994*, p. 443.

- America's merchandise trade balance has been negative every year since 1976, running at a negative annual level between \$100 and \$150B since 1985.[5] Since 1980, the annual federal deficit has quadrupled from \$73B to over \$290B.[6]

- The United States is now the largest debtor nation in the world.[7] 21 percent of our annual federal budget is used to pay the interest on our \$4.1 trillion debt.[8] To pay off the national debt today would cost each and every American family more than \$60,000!

- In 1980, Japan passed the United States as the number-one automaker—exceeding U.S. production by 40 percent.

- In 1970, the United States dominated consumer electronics. In 1991, we produced approximately 13 percent of this \$100B industry.[9]

- The top three electronics companies in the number of U.S. patents issued in 1991 were Toshiba, Hitachi, and Mitsubishi.[10]

- U.S. SAT scores have dropped significantly over the past 20 years. In 1967, the average score was 958. Today it's 899.[11] U.S. students of Asian extraction had the highest average SAT scores in 1992 (at 927).[12]

---

[5]ibid., p. 790.

[6]ibid., p. 328.

[7]R. Battra, *The Great Depression of 1990* (Simon & Schuster, 1987), p. 140.

[8]*The American Almanac 1993–1994*, p. 333.

[9]*Electronics in the World* (Electronics International Corporation, New York, Nov. 1991), p. 40.

[10]"Protecting the Power of the Idea," *Electronic Business*, p. 24–32, Feb. 1992.

[11]*The American Almanac 1993–1994*, p. 170.

[12]"SAT Scores Show Signs of Recovery," *USA Today*, p. D1, Aug. 27, 1992.

- Between 1989 and 1992, Japanese investors purchased equity in 426 U.S. high-tech companies. In approximately the same time frame, the United States made only 94 investments in Japanese companies—and most of these were under conditions where the United States did not receive access to Japanese technology.[13]

- The largest commercial bank in the United States is Citicorp, with assets of $213 billion. It is the 27th largest bank in the world, with the top eight being Japanese.[14]

In the automotive industry, the United States has been struggling mightily to recover its one-time leadership. The differences between Japanese and U.S. auto plants were cited in a classic study in 1990[15] and are illustrated in Table 1.1. In particular, note the difference between the productivity of Japanese-owned plants located in the United States and traditional U.S. auto plants (the data enclosed by the circles). In both cases, the workers were from the United States but the management style, as well as much of the equipment and supplies for the Japanese-owned plant, came from Japan. Although the productivity was higher and the defects and absenteeism lower for the U.S.-based Japanese plant, the performance of both U.S.-based plants was not as good as for the one located in Japan. Through quality-focused manufacturing and quicker product-to-market times, U.S. automakers have reduced these differences over the past several years, but they have not yet disappeared.

As a result of their unswerving focus on manufacturing quality and consumer satisfaction, Japan's automotive in-

---

[13]"Japanese Know-how Now Easier for the U.S. to Acquire," *R&D Magazine*, p. 85–86, Apr. 1993.

[14]"Fortune Guide to the Global Service," *Fortune*, p. 165, August 23, 1993.

[15]James P. Womack, Daniel T. Jones, and Daniel Roos, *The Machine that Changed the World* (Harper Perennial, New York, 1991) p. 92.

TABLE 1.1.   Productivity, defects, and absenteeism for automobile manufacturing facilities located in the United States, Japan, and Europe.

	Japan	Japanese plants in U.S.	U.S. plants in U.S.	Europe
Productivity (hours per vehicle)	16.8	21.2	25.1	36.2
Assembly defects (per 100 autos)	60	65	82	97
Absenteeism (percentage)	5.0	4.8	11.7	12.1

SOURCE: Table prepared with data extracted from James P. Womack, Daniel T. Jones, and Daniel Roos, "The Machine that Changed the World: The Story of Lean Production" (Rawson Associates, New York, 1990). Courtesy of MIT International Motor Vehicle Program.

dustry has grown dramatically over the past 30 years, as shown in Figure 1.2. Note that automobile production in the United States has been approximately constant at 10 to 12 million vehicles annually since 1965. Before 1960, the auto industry in Japan was virtually nonexistent; however, by 1980, Japan had become the largest auto builder in the world, outproducing the United States by 5 to 20 percent each subsequent year. In 1994, in the face of a severe recession in Japan, it appears that the United States will surpass Japan in automobile production for the first time in 14 years!

In several other important industries, Japan has overtaken U.S. technology leadership. For example in the electronics industry, the United States has been running a world trade deficit of $5 to $15B annually since 1984. This imbalance arises primarily from imports from Japan and Korea, where companies such as Sharp, Canon, Sony, Samsung, Mitsubishi, NEC, and Goldstar have become household brand names, associated with reliable, leading-edge products.

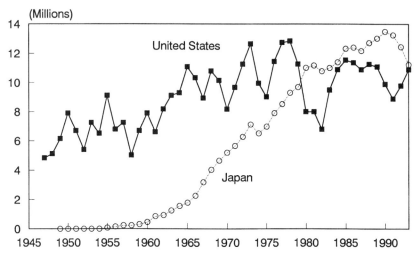

FIGURE 1.2.   Automobile production for the United States and Japan, 1947 through 1992.
SOURCE: Courtesy of *Automotive News*.

One electronics area has become especially important for continued U.S. economic progress: semiconductor integrated circuits. These serve as the heart of virtually all advanced electronic products, and most of the progress in electronics over the past three decades has come about primarily through semiconductor improvements. For example, today's memory chips are nearly 1,000 times less expensive per bit than their ancestors of 15 years ago. Steady advances like this for the $80B semiconductor industry drive the growth of the $800B worldwide electronics industry!

Recognizing the importance of semiconductors to the general electronics industry, we can examine the U.S. presence in the semiconductor market. In Figure 1.3, we see the overall decline that has occurred following our once-dominant position in the mid-'70s. Quite encouraging is the general flattening (and reversal) of this curve over the past three years, much of which can be attributed to the new business/technology paradigm that is being embraced across America. However, a subtle factor in the data of Figure 1.3 lies in the fact that DRAMs—the memory elements for most computers—are the major (high-volume)

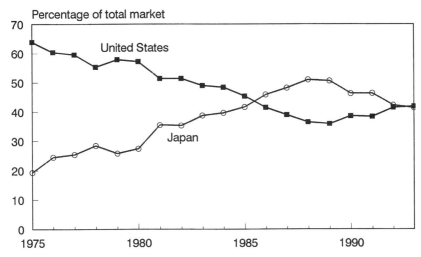

**FIGURE 1.3. Worldwide market share for U.S. and Japanese
semiconductor manufacturers, 1975 through 1993.**
SOURCE: Courtesy of Dataquest.

technology drivers for the entire semiconductor industry,
and strong Pacific-rim leadership in this area threatens future U.S. semiconductor manufacturing.

The same trend indicated in Figure 2.3 has occurred
throughout many markets that constitute the electronics
food chain—from materials to processing equipment to
semiconductor products to electronic equipment and systems. In each market segment, Japanese high-technology
suppliers have gradually wrestled market shares from U.S.
companies. We are now involved in a horse race of gigan-
tic proportions, with business survival as the winner's tro-
phy. As shown in Figure 1.4, the materials and equipment
processing markets are relatively small ($10B) but feed the
larger semiconductor components business ($80B) and the
U.S.'s largest manufacturing sector, electronics ($800B).
Figure 1.5 illustrates the extent to which the U.S. position in
several other electronics-related markets has eroded over
the past three decades.

Particularly distressing to technologists is the possibil-
ity of the United States losing its long-standing leadership
in emerging technologies. Most experts feel that we have

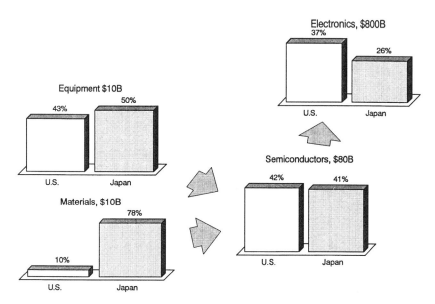

FIGURE 1.4.   Japanese penetration of the electronic food chain.*

*Percentages represent worldwide market share by country of ownership.

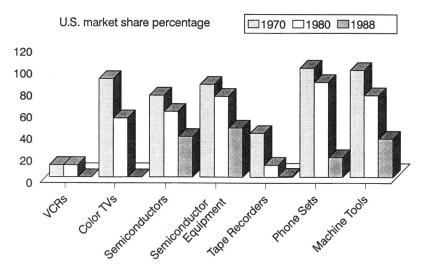

FIGURE 1.5.   Erosion of U.S. market share in selected technical industries.

SOURCE: Council on Competitiveness, "Picking up the Pace," 1988.

the finest R&D establishments in the world—ranging from our research universities (University of California-Berkeley, MIT, Stanford, University of Illinois) to our corporate R&D Centers (IBM, GE, Xerox, DuPont). However, the United States is losing significant ground in R&D in several important areas:

- Many of our once-great industrial research centers have been altered or divested (Bell Laboratories and RCA Laboratories), while others have been gradually redirected toward shorter-term product development (Tektronix, Amoco, General Electric, IBM).

- We are simply not investing enough in non-defense R&D relative to that of our global competitors (see Figure 1.6).

- Whatever advantages are gained in R&D are often lost to more nimble foreign competitors during the commercialization cycle (Table 1.2).

FIGURE 1.6.   Total public and private-sector non-defense R&D investment.
SOURCE: Data extracted from Science and Engineering Indicators—1993, Appendix Table 4-36, p. 376.

TABLE 1.2. Relative standing of the United States and Japan in emerging technologies.

	R&D	Trends	Product Introductions	Trends
Advanced materials	Even	[down arrow]	[Japan]	[down arrow]
Advanced semiconductors	Even	Even	[Japan]	[down arrow]
Artificial intelligence	[U.S. flag]	Even	[U.S. flag]	Even
Biotechnology	[U.S. flag]	[down arrow]	[U.S. flag]	[down arrow]
Digital imaging	Even	[down arrow]	[Japan]	[down arrow]
Computer integrated manufacturing	[U.S. flag]	Even	Even	Even
High-density data storage	Even	Even	[Japan]	[down arrow]
High-performance computing	[U.S. flag]	Even	[U.S. flag]	[down arrow]
Medical diagnostics	[U.S. flag]	Even	[U.S. flag]	[down arrow]
Optoelectronics	Even	Even	[Japan]	[down arrow]
Sensors	[U.S. flag]	[down arrow]	Even	Even
Superconductors	Even	[down arrow]	Even	[down arrow]

Key: The downward arrow indicates that the trend is down for the United States.

SOURCE: Data is from the U.S. Dept. of Commerce and the National Institute of Standards and Technology, and is provided through the courtesy of the Industrial Research Institute. *Research Technology Management*, vol. 33, p. 4, Sept.–Oct. 1990. Courtesy of the Industrial Research Institute.

- Even our universities have begun shifting toward short-term or applied projects, in order to capture industry support in the light of diminishing federal defense funding. This is discussed further in chapter 11.

The relative R&D investment in non-defense programs in the United States (Figure 1.6) has significantly lagged that of our two fiercest economic competitors (Germany and Japan) over the past two decades. Admittedly, defense-related R&D is not included in this figure, and some fraction of the large U.S. military investment surely trickles down to non-defense applications. Nonetheless, in direct funding of commercial R&D, the size of the U.S. investment does not speak of leadership.

Regarding product commercialization, we have simply been outmarketed by the customer-driven approach of the Japanese. As shown in Table 1.2, even emerging areas in which the United States has an undisputed lead in R&D often fall to the Japanese when the technology reaches the product commercialization stage. In every technology cited in Table 1.2, the United States is either losing (or at best holding) relative to the Japanese. In no cases is it catching up or extending its lead.

The seriousness of the U.S. technology erosion is even more evident when we examine the recent accomplishments of our major competitor. Among industrial nations, Japan is attributed to having the following distinctions:[16]

- The lowest unemployment rate in the world.
- World leadership in patents.
- The largest percentage of scientists and engineers in the workforce.
- The highest ranking scholastic test scores in math and science.
- The highest percentage of students completing high school.
- The highest literacy rate.
- The highest life expectancy.
- The lowest crime rate.
- The toughest pollution control standards.
- Ownership of 8 of the 10 world's largest banks.

Finally, despite the foreign competition's rapid growth in science and engineering, the U.S. awareness of technology trends that occur across the oceans is embarrassing. International technical conferences that are held in the

---

[16]Taken mostly from Peter B. Grazier, *Before It's too Late* (Teambuilding, Inc., Chadds Ford, PA, 1989), p. 21.

United States attract legions of foreign scientists who have notepads (or cameras) in hand and are eager to learn about any recent advances. Similar conferences held in Japan are fortunate to be attended by a handful of U.S. participants. Japanese visits to U.S. research centers and universities are frequent, and the foreign scientists are usually well aware of their host's developments, as reported at conferences and in technical journals. In contrast, tight travel budgets and management skepticism limit U.S. visitors to Japanese research communities. A report released by Japan's Science and Technology Agency[17] cited 69,000 annual visits to the United States by Japanese researchers, but only 5,000 visits to Japan from U.S. researchers!

From any perspective, a change in the U.S. technology game plan is long overdue. Fortunately, many U.S. companies have been addressing new ways of doing business (and developing successful products) head on and are adapting successfully to the global economy. We have seen how the semiconductor and automotive industries have recently progressed against Japanese competition. Part of their success is due to a deep Japanese recessionary cycle and to a devalued yen. But another part is due to the changes invoked in aggressive U.S. companies that have adapted the new development and business ways. This book describes that paradigm for technology and product development. Only by embracing such change can the United States hope to remain an important factor in the global economy of tomorrow.

IN SUMMARY

The United States has slipped from being the world's dominant manufacturing and technology leader in the '50s and '60s to being a service-based country and the world's largest debtor nation in the '80s and '90s. Over the past 20

---

[17]"Japanese Know-how Now Easier for the U.S. to Acquire," op. cit., p. 86.

years, we have witnessed the erosion of U.S. leadership in consumer electronics, automobiles, steel, lumber, and textiles. In these, and in critical technologies such as semiconductors, flat-panel displays, and computers, we are engaged in an economic fight for survival. While the United States has unequivocally assumed the role as the world's military and political superpower, its traditional position in the global marketplace is in jeopardy.

Some companies have been quick to recognize the time for change and have made the necessary business modifications to meet international competition. As we will show in subsequent chapters, a major part of these changes has to do with the way we bring our products to market—from concept to commercialization, from research to actualization. There is a better way!

CHAPTER 2

Product

Development

Although it is overly simplistic to advocate a single theme to revitalize U.S. technology, I do suggest one compelling direction that is at least necessary, if not sufficient. The clearest hope for the continued economic leadership of the United States lies in improving the overall effectiveness of its product and technology development process. Such an approach does not dwell on past or current products; for them, the die has already been cast. Their inherent strengths or weaknesses will determine the success of our commerce for the next one to three years. Improvements in the product and technology development process, however, will impact the next several generations of products—and it is there we should concentrate.

> The good news is that some segments of the U.S. industry have already begun making dramatic changes in the product and technology development process. The bad news is that so many others haven't.

Regarding the importance of product and technology development, consider a survey on the product-innovation process carried out by Arthur D. Little.[1] This survey probed leaders (75 percent CEOs, presidents, and vice-presidents) from 701 companies around the world (50 percent Europe, 40 percent U.S., and 10 percent Japan). Every respondent indicated significant effort in their company to improve the product-innovation process. Figure 2.1 illustrates their responses as to where their company is putting its major efforts. Two of the first four responses ("getting new products to market on schedule" and "developing new products faster") are directly related to faster product and technology development. We will show later in this book that all of the other responses are also related to the new technology development paradigm.

The importance of developing new products and technology faster was underscored in a classic study, "Speeding

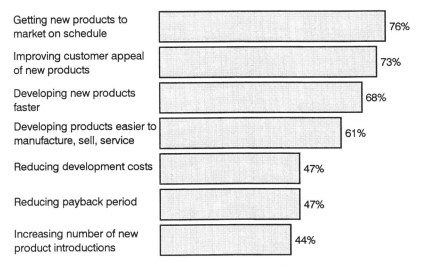

FIGURE 2.1.   Survey on the Product Innovation Process.
*Responses indicate areas where companies are putting their major efforts to improve the process.
SOURCE: *The Arthur D. Little Survey on the Product Innovation Process* (Cambridge, MA, December 1991, p. 6. Courtesy of Arthur D. Little).

---

[1]*The Arthur D. Little Survey on the Product Innovation Process* (Arthur D. Little, Cambridge, MA, 1991), p. 6.

Up Product Development," by McKinsey and Company.[2] In this study, several problems that might occur during product development were modeled, and their impact on after-tax profits calculated. The study showed that overrunning development costs by 50 percent had only a 3.5 percent negative impact on profits, but that overrunning the development schedule by six months produced a 33 percent negative impact (see Figure 2.2). Such a major impact of a delay in product development is not difficult to understand when we illustrate the life cycle curve of a fictitious product (Figure 2.3). Here, we assume three-year start up, maturity, and declining phases. A one-year delay in development would cause the revenue loss depicted by the shaded region, since the onset of the maturity phase and the declining phase would almost certainly be fixed by external market

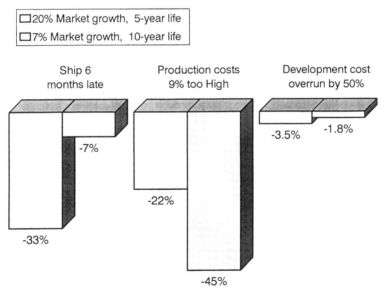

FIGURE 2.2. Results of a McKinsey study of product development problems and their impact on after-tax profitability.
SOURCE: Courtesy of McKinsey and Company, New York.

[2]D. G. Reinertsen, "Whodunit? The Search for the New-Product Killers," *Electronic Business,* July 1983.

FIGURE 2.3. Fictitious product life cycle curve, illustrating lost revenue due to a one-year delay in product introduction.

conditions. The example in Figure 2.3 produces nearly a 40 percent loss in sales and presumably a similar loss in profits over the life of the product.

> Reduce product development time to one third, and you will triple profits and triple growth.[3]

Rapid product and technology development also provides several indirect benefits:

- Early products bring higher profit margins than those subsequently introduced—when competition is stiffer.

- Early products are more apt to meet customer needs. Such needs, when determined during the product-

---

[3]"The Quality Imperative," *Business Week Bonus Issue*, Oct. 25, 1991, p. 14.

definition phase of the development, will shift with time and soon be addressed by other methods (or products).

- Suppliers who can respond to the market quickly can provide a variety of products, thereby sampling the dynamic marketplace more frequently for trends.

- Early products are more apt to capture large market shares, thereby increasing their product life, as well as the probability of becoming *de facto* market standards.

An organization that can provide a customer with a portfolio of new models—featuring the latest solutions to current problems—is most apt to be successful. For example, the rapid (46-month) development cycles in Japan's auto industry between 1982 and 1990 allowed it to provide potential customers with nearly twice as many different models at any given time than U.S. automakers (with their 60-month development cycle). As illustrated in Figure 2.4, the same capability also allows a supplier to turn its inventories

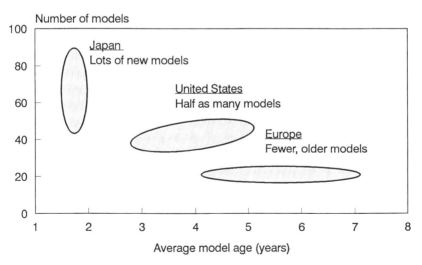

FIGURE 2.4. Number of auto models and age of models existing in a given year for U.S., Japanese, and European auto manufacturers.
SOURCE: James P. Womack, Daniel T. Jones, and Daniel Roos, "The Machine that Changed the World." Courtesy of International Motor Vehicle Program.

quickly, replacing older models with more attractive (newer) models. It is not difficult to imagine how this appeals to consumers and promotes additional sales revenue.

> Time is not only money—it's an awful lot of money.

Many industry leaders are quite outspoken about the need to improve our product development process:

> "We've ignored a critical success factor: speed. Our competitors abroad have turned new technologies into new products and processes more rapidly. And they've reaped the commercial rewards of the time-to-market race."[4]
> —*John Young,*
> *former CEO, Hewlett Packard Corp.*
>
> "We came to the realization that if you get to market sooner with new technology, you can charge a premium until the others follow."[5]
> —*John Hanley,*
> *vice-president of product development, AT&T*
>
> "The long-term objective for growth is going to be satisfied only by successful new product programs, and we must get on with the process of reducing the time to bring new product offerings to market."[6]
> —*Jack T. Hartley,*
> *chairman/CEO, Harris Corp.*

---

[4]B. Dumaine, "How Managers Can Succeed Through Speed," *Fortune,* Feb. 13, 1989.

[5]ibid.

[6]Harris Operational Effectiveness Conference, Melbourne, FL, Nov. 1989.

> "Doing it fast forces you to do it [product develop-
> ment] right the first time."
> *—John Young,*
> *former CEO, Hewlett Packard Corp.*
>
> "What we dislike most about bigness is that it too
> often generates slowness. We have seen what
> wins in our marketplaces around the globe:
> speed, speed, and more speed."[7]
> *—Jack Welch,*
> *CEO, General Electric*

A final endorsement of the critical need for improved product and technology can be found in three advertisements taken from *Electronic Business* magazine. The first (Figure 2.5a,) from Xilinx,[8] asks: "How much is it worth to get to market first," and continues with, "The value of timely market entry is no longer incalculable. Research shows that a six month delay in getting to market reduces a product's profitability by a third over its life cycle."

The second (Figure 2.5b), from Sun Microsystems (an engineering workstation manufacturer) and Cadence Design Systems (a software CAD system vendor),[9] states: "If there's one thing we at Cadence and Sun understand, it's your need to ship product before the next guy." It continues, "Faster (circuit) simulation and layout are a good start. But finishing first depends on accelerating your entire (product) design process, front to back."

Finally, from Vicor comes the third ad (Figure 2.6) that starts with: "Opportunity Lost," and goes on to state,

---

[7]GE Quarterly Report, Second Quarter 1993, August 1993.

[8]*Electronic Business*, April 27, 1992, p. 20.

[9]ibid., p. 54

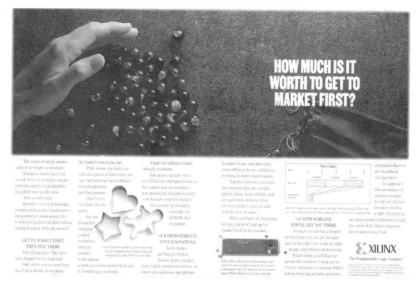

a. Xilinx

b. Sun/Cadence

FIGURE 2.5. Advertisements appearing in *Electronic Business*, April 27, 1992.

"Time to market . . . Get there late and the consequences are inevitable."[10] The creatures in this ad seemed to have missed their window of opportunity and suffered the fate of extinction. The analogy to the business world is obvious. Just as manufacturing and quality were the themes of the '80s—so too will product development be that of the '90s.

---

[10]*Electronic Business,* June 1992. p. 26.

Time to market...Get there late and the consequences are inevitable.

You want the shortest path to successful product development, but all too often the system power supply becomes a stumbling block. Development delays, safety agency approvals, EMI/RFI testing, size problems, cooling issues, cost overruns, last minute changes in power requirements and manufacturing disasters, and you've missed your market opportunity.

Your sales drift toward the competition, and your product toward extinction.

Vicor's families of agency-approved modular power components and complete power systems provide proven, high performance solutions to virtually any power problem — from watts to kilowatts – in a fraction of the space required by conventional solutions.

Give us a call...with off-the-shelf availability and overnight delivery...you won't have to wait 40 days and 40 nights to get your system up and running.

Component Solutions For Your Power System

23 Frontage Road, Andover, MA 01810
TEL: (508) 470-2900 • FAX: (508) 475-6715

FIGURE 2.6. An advertisement appearing in *Electronic Business*, April 27, 1992.
SOURCE: Courtesy of Vicor, Andover MA.

IN SUMMARY

In several recent studies, quick market entry has been found to be the single most important factor for commercial profitability. For example, the McKinsey team showed that a delay of six months in completing the product development cycle can reduce after-tax profits by 33 percent. Short product development cycles also mean that a supplier can respond to market dynamics quickly—offering a greater range of products and improving the likelihood of meeting the customer's needs. Surprisingly (at first), speeding up the development cycle does not mean making more mistakes; it means doing things right the first time. And it doesn't increase costs—it decreases them!

In response to many of the problems indicated in the first two chapters, dramatic changes have begun to sweep across the U.S. industrial community. One of the most significant changes is that related to the manner in which we develop new products and technologies. Most major U.S. corporations recognize the need for change and the importance of addressing the *process* associated with product and technology development. However, the overall directions of these programs vary significantly from company to company, and even between organizations within the same company. In the next several chapters, we examine the major components of this new development process and successful approaches for its implementation.

CHAPTER 3

The

People

HISTORICAL PERSPECTIVE

The United States has led world commerce and technology since the Industrial Revolution. Led by the invention of the transistor at Bell Laboratories, Americans gave birth to modern-day electronics and the solid-state revolution. In the early '50s, RCA so monopolized television, that it was forced by the U.S. government to relinquish most of its intellectual property rights to other companies. Consumer electronics was the dominion of giants such as GE, RCA, Zenith, Westinghouse, Emerson, Philco, and Sylvania. Everyone drove Chevys and Fords. From such dominance, an environment of complacency and entitlement began to set upon the average American worker. It was led by powerful trade unions and tolerated by professionals who rode their shirt tails for similar benefit packages. The rallying cry became: What's in it for me?

A classic study by Theodore H. Barry Associates in the late 1970s showed that the typical eight-hour work day of a five-day work week for U.S. workers at that time could be divided into the following elements:[1]

---

[1]Described by H. Garrett DeYoung, "Making R&D Pay Off Better and Quicker," *Electronic Business*, p. 61–64, Dec. 1992.

Time used productively:	4.4 hours
Time lost due to personal and unavoidable delays:	1.2 hours
Time just wasted:	2.4 hours

Compare this to the six-day work week, 10 to 14 hour work day, and vacation give-backs in Japan!

The attitude of the American worker was also nurtured by a management approach that separated the general work force from management. The brainchild of Frederick Taylor,[2] this management style prevailed in the United States (and much of the Western world) from the early 1900s through perhaps 1980. Taylor's methods promoted separation of management and workers, individual incentives for individual performance, engineering and manufacturing void of human complications, and an analytic, bottom-up approach that broke complex problems into small, manageable segments. Overall, it served western society well for three-fourths of the twentieth century. However, its limitations began to appear as the need for teamwork grew at the expense of the individual. According to W. Edwards Deming, the world-renown quality expert, the Taylor-oriented U.S. management system "crushes motivation, self-esteem, dignity and eagerness to learn." It ranks workers by production quotas and annual appraisals. The resulting corporate culture "encourages competition—not collaboration."[3]

Most important, Taylorism promoted managers as the thinkers and all other employees as the doers, breeding slogans such as: "Hey, I just work here" and "That's not my job."

---

[2]J. E. Gibson, "Foundations of World-Class Manufacturing Systems," National Academy of Engineering, 1991. Also, "Taylorism and Professional Education," The Bent of Tau Beta Pi, Fall 1991, p. 14–18.

[3]As described in *Focus* (National Center for Manufacturing Sciences, Ann Arbor, MI, Mar. 1993), p. 1.

Konosuke Matsushita, the late leader of the giant Matsushita Corporation, made the following comments in a speech to American businessmen:[4]

"We are going to win and the industrial West is going to lose out. There's not much you can do about it because the reasons for your failure are within yourselves. Your firms are built on the (Frederick) Taylor model. Even worse, so are your heads."

The adversarial role between labor and management, combined with the general complacency that came with long-term industrial domination has bred a culture of entitlement, with our work force advocating individual benefits—whether or not they are deserved or affordable. In the last few years, American workers have come to realize the direct and highly personal links between employee productivity, customer satisfaction, and job security. Like it or not, surviving in today's high-technology business society is everyone's job. No one is entitled.

A final but important factor that shapes the nature of American workers is their upbringing as strong individualists. The United States was founded by such leaders. The success of its frontiersmen and early industrialists stemmed largely from powerful convictions, determination, and personal leadership. Such characteristics have always been our strength—but in today's more complex technological world, they are also our weakness. No single mind, no matter how brilliant, can absorb all the intricacies of electronic systems containing billions of active elements and their thermal and electrical interactions. To comprehend just the instruction manuals associated with a modern avionics system would take a single engineer an appreciable part of his or her career.

---

[4]L. A. Fitzgerald, "How to Fail-Proof TQM: The Art of Organizational Transformation," *Transactions of the 14th Annual AQP Spring Conference and Resource Mart* (Association for Quality and Participation, Cincinnati, OH, 1992), p. 466.

The world has changed, and the time of the rugged individualist has passed.

> None of us is as smart as all of us![5]

Confident of its accomplishments but stunned by the economic turns of the past decade, the American work force wants to do better. Most Americans are underutilized and anxious for the chance to make a difference. Although their work place is frantic, and they're always busy, they seem to be walking up a down escalator. There has to be a better way—and there is.

WORK TEAMS

Traditionally, product or technology development has been done through separate departments of specialists who are believed to be able to maintain their expertise only through close day-to-day association with others in the same specialty. Hence, there is a design department, a process development group, a manufacturing organization, quality assurance, sales, and so on. Each has its own requirements, procedures, sign-offs, and transfer procedures. In this culture, product development requires a champion who is able to master the group interfaces through a combination of diplomacy, intimidation, and outright pleading. The transitions are handled sequentially, with few specialists extending very far outside their own department.

The whole process can be visualized by a set of islands, each representing a specific department with bridges between each island. The bridges are of many types—some fragile, some smooth, and some broken. A product champion must travel across the series of islands to reach the marketplace, and cross many bridges (and communities) in the process. It is an arduous and lengthy journey at best!

---

[5]Peter B. Grazier, *Before It's Too Late*, op. cit., p. 165.

Some companies have found a better way: self-directed work teams. Of 582 CEOs surveyed by *Electronic Business*, 76 percent named employee involvement as the single, best way to improve product quality.[6] In Arthur D. Little's product innovation survey of 701 companies, self-directed work teams were the only approach that had been adapted by a majority of the respondents (actually 85 percent reported trying it in their companies). Moreover, of the 85 percent who tried such teams, 61.6 percent rated its success high in improving the product innovation process. This was the highest response indicated, as shown in Figure 3.1. Some of our top industry leaders have endorsed empowered work teams:

> "The winners in the next few decades will be the companies with the most empowered work teams."
> —*Michael Dell,*
> *CEO, Dell Computer*
>
> "The heroic style—the lone cowboy on horseback—is not the figure we worship anymore at Apple. Now, teams are heroes."[7]
> —*John Scully,*
> *former CEO, Apple Computer*

The following commentary came from a full-page advertisement in USA Today on October 14, 1991 that Chrysler ran when it announced the opening of its new automotive R&D center in Detroit:

> "No more piece-by-piece, step-by-step production. Now it's teams. Teams of product and manufacturing engineers, designers, planners, financing and marketing people—together from the start . . . It's how we built Dodge Viper . . . from dream to showroom in three years, a record

---

[6]*Electronic Business*, Oct. 17, 1991

[7]R. M. Kanter, *When Giants Learn to Dance* (Simon & Schuster, 1989), p. 51.

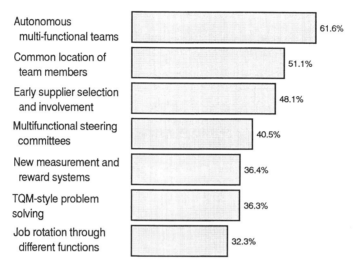

FIGURE 3.1. Success rate for different approaches to enhance the product innovation process.
SOURCE: *The Arthur D. Little Survey on the Product Innovation Process*, p. 12. Courtesy of Arthur D. Little.

for U.S. car makers. From now on, all our cars and trucks will be higher quality, built at lower cost and delivered to the market faster. That's what competition is all about."

For industrial product development, a multifunctional work team should be made up of employees from sales, marketing, design engineering, product engineering, manufacturing and quality. Two other team members from outside the company are key customers and suppliers (Figure 3.2). These partners are often overlooked in the United States, but they can be extremely important allies. In Japan, supplier-customer partnerships are formed through huge *keiretsus*—long-term alliances that encompass a broad range of business interests.

To describe the power of the Japanese keiretsu system further, Table 3.1 lists the major companies that belong to the DKB keiretsu—one of eight major keiretsu families that account for 78 percent of the value of all shares on the

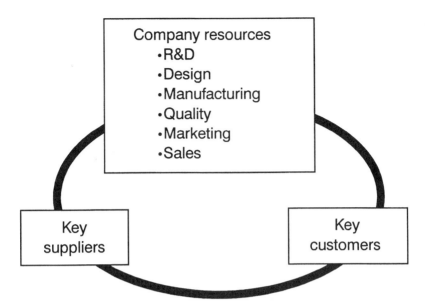

FIGURE 3.2. The multifunctional work team for product and technology development.

Tokyo Stock Exchange.[8] Japanese merchants are very closely involved with their keiretsu partners; company executives meet regularly to discuss the nature of their relationship and mutual business opportunities. Many of these relationships have existed for several generations. The Japanese almost always purchase supplies and services from keiretsu partners; only if their needs can clearly not be met through such a relationship, will they consider purchasing outside the keiretsu. Although such a network does not exist in the United States, strong relationships can be built through the participation of major customers and suppliers in the product development process.

In a team-oriented environment, it is not necessary for all team members to participate full time in a single product development project, nor must they all participate

---

[8]C. Rappoport, "Why Japan Keeps on Winning," *Fortune*, p. 76–85, July 15, 1991.

TABLE 3.1. Major companies in the DKB keiretsu family in Japan.

Industry	Companies	
Financial services	• Dai-Chi Kangyo Bank • Asahi Mutual Life • Taisei Fire and Marine • Fukoku Mutual Life	• Nissan Fire and Marine • Kankaku Securities • Orient
Computers and electronics	• Fujitsu • Fuji Electric • Yaskawa Electric Mfg.	• Nippon Columbia • Hitachi
Cars	• Isuzu Motors	
Trading and retailing	• Itoh • Nissho Iwa	• Kanamatsu • Seibu Department Stores
Construction	• Shimizu	
Metals	• Kawasaki Steel • Kobe Steel • Japan Metals and Chemicals	• Nippon Light Metal • Furukawa • Furukawa Electric
Real estate	• Tokyo Dome	
Oil and coal	• Showa Shell Sekiyu	
Rubber and glass	• Yokohama Rubber	
Chemicals	• Kyowa Hakko Kogyo • Denki Kagaku Kogyo • Nippon Zeon • Asahi Denka Kogyo	• Sankyo • Shiseido • Lion
Fibers and textiles	• Asahi Chemical Industry	
Pulp and paper	• Honshu Paper	

Industrial equipment	• Nigata Engineering
	• Iseki
	• Ebara
		• Kawasaki Heavy
		  Industries
		• Isikawajima-Harima
		  Heavy Industries

Camera and optics	• Asahi Optical	
Cement	• Chichibu Cement	
Shipping and transportation	• Kawasaki Kisen • Shibusawa Warehouse	• Nippon Express

SOURCE: "Why Japan Keeps on Winning," *Fortune*, July 15, 1991, p. 76–85.

equally. However, they should share in important team events and communications, so that each member is on top of the critical issues and opportunities and is able to step in as needed to provide special capabilities. Compared to the islands of individual departments and the broken bridges, the members of self-directed work teams (including the major customer) should pile into a single vehicle and proceed toward the marketplace as a team. The vehicle must still travel through the functional communities, but the team members now have the expertise and skills among themselves to anticipate and handle the necessary customs and interfaces. Moreover, the departments themselves are now quite different, since most of their former members are now serving on other teams. The entire development culture has become project oriented.

One of the most important benefits of empowered work teams is their ability to carry out development concurrently. Concurrent development is the process by which multifunctional work teams combine expertise and efforts to carry out as many of the steps in the development process as possible *in parallel*, thereby minimizing the overall development time and maximizing the chances for commercial product success.

The major advantage such a team has to concurrently develop a product is its ability to anticipate (and resolve in advance) the many tactical problems that will be confronted over the course of the project.

Takeuchi and Nonaka[9] have described the traditional development process as a relay race, with its totally sequential methodology. In contrast, they depict concurrent development as a rugby scrimmage, with dynamic interplay between team members leading to downward field motion and a "goal."

Simply speaking, the concurrent work team has two familiar objectives within the framework of its mission:

---

[9]H. Takeuchi and I. Nonaka, "The New New Product Development Game," *Harvard Business Review*, p. 137–146, Jan.–Feb. 1986.

- To define the right product.

- To design, develop, and market the product right.

The first objective determines the eventual success of the product in the marketplace. The second ensures that it gets there on time, on budget, and with the agreed-upon functionality and quality.

Producing the right product (or technology) does not get sufficient attention in traditional U.S. development practices. By the right product, we mean one that is synchronized with the organization's overall strategic direction; it is defined with extensive participation of major customers (whether internal or external) to ensure that it will meet their needs; the organization's technology, manufacturing, and marketing resources are in place to support it; and it has been analyzed with regard to manufacturability so that it can be produced at a competitive cost. In the United States, considerable attention is given to doing a project right (efficiently), but rather feeble efforts are often made to ensure that the product itself is the right one (profitable). Fortunately, this weakness is beginning to be recognized.

Within the framework of doing the right product and doing the product right, the work team has several specific objectives, including:

- Working with major customers and internal marketing and business leaders to define a product that meets the customer needs and market competition cost-effectively.

- Anticipating manufacturing issues (including component processing, assembly, and testing), and designing the product to minimize them.

- Preparing a business plan that establishes the expected revenues, costs, and timing. Informing management early in the development cycle, if the primary goals cannot be met.

- Minimizing product-to-market time, thereby reducing development costs and ensuring the earliest possible market entry.

An illustration of the manner in which concurrent team members with different functional capabilities participate throughout the several phases of product development is presented in Figure 3.3. This shows the heavy effort required of strategic marketing and planning functions in the beginning of the project, design engineering in the middle, and manufacturing and product marketing near the end. But the transitions are gradual, without abrupt hand-offs or changes of responsibility.

There are many differences in responsibility between the traditional development approach and that used for

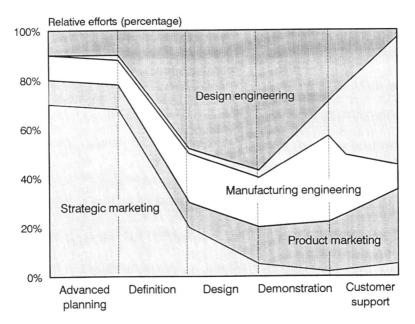

FIGURE 3.3.   Relative effort expended by various functional team members as a program progresses through the five phases of product or technology development.
(Data is illustrative only.)
SOURCE: Courtesy of Harris Corporation, Melbourne, FL.

TABLE 3.2. A comparison of the role of employees and managers in traditional and team-oriented product and technology development.

Topic	Traditional	Team
Job categories	Many	Few
Job breadth	Narrow	Broad
Authority	Management	Team
Rewards	Individual performance and seniority	Team performance

SOURCE: J. D. Orsburn et al., *Self-Directed Work Teams: The New American Challenge* (Business One Irwin, Homewood, IL, 1990) p. 11.

concurrent, team-oriented development. As illustrated in Table 3.2, team-oriented concurrent development provides each employee with a broader role and larger responsibility in determining the success of the project.

ELEMENTS OF A SUCCESSFUL WORK TEAM

An engineer or scientist is first and foremost an individualist. He or she has generally been rewarded throughout the school years for individual accomplishment. In many schools, teamwork has not only been avoided, it has been discouraged. For those attending graduate school, the fear of a thesis project not meeting the requirement of originality underscores individual work habits. University faculty members themselves are products of and contributors to such a system in their competitive quest for publications and R&D contracts. Our graduating engineers and scientists have been trained and rewarded in a strongly individualistic work ethic and therefore must adapt to the team-oriented approach necessary in today's high-technology, industrial environment.

There are six essential ingredients of a work team. These are listed in Table 3.3, and discussed further in the following sections.

TABLE 3.3.   Essential ingredients of a self-directed work team.

1. The team must be given a **clear and beneficial goal**.
2. It must be **empowered** to carry out all tactical activities.
3. Members of the team must be **trained or experienced** in team dynamics.
4. The goal and efforts must be given visible **management recognition and support**.
5. Progress must be **measured** against agreed-upon expectations.
6. The team must be located and interconnected in such a way to promote **frequent informal communications** between team members.

Clear goal and objectives

Expectations must be stated very clearly. As early as possible, the few major objectives or marketing message for the planned product must be determined and communicated, making sure that all team members clearly understand the message as well as the importance of its attainment. Once communicated, the message should not be changed lightly.

In large organizations, communications go awry easily, and special efforts must be made to avoid misunderstandings. The best method is to convey the goal, in specific measurable terms, directly to the entire work team. This is the major responsibility of management and is especially effective if first communicated by a senior executive. Clarity in the team's mission is then assured, and the importance of the team and the project is effectively underscored by the executive's personal kick-off.

In specifying the objectives, it is also essential for management to communicate any strategic boundary conditions, such as the completion time (to meet a market window) or a product manufacturing cost (to meet a target application). For example, the first solid-state portable calculator was the HP-35, which was introduced by Hewlett Packard in the mid-'70s. It is said that Bill Hewlett demanded of the project team that the final product be small enough to fit in an engineer's jacket pocket. Such a boundary condition was critical to the overall commercial success of the product and was correctly stated as a challenge to the project team in its goal. The team could make all sorts of trade-offs in getting to the final product, but in the end—it had to be able to fit in an engineer's pocket! Period.

Lack of a clear, well-understood goal is the single greatest cause of failure for a product or technology development team. If the team, after planning and further defining the project in detail, cannot meet the goal (within the specified set of boundary conditions), it must indicate this to top management as early as possible in the development process. It is then the responsibility of management (with the help of the team), to revise the original objectives or to cancel the project. But what is not acceptable under any conditions is for the team, on their own, to alter the goal or the boundary conditions—that goes beyond empowerment because it affects the overall strategic direction of the organization.

Finally, the goal for a successful work team must be communicated by management and perceived by the team as important to the organization. Development of a product or technology that is thought to serve a dead-end market or to be assigned primarily as a stop-gap management tactic will be only weakly endorsed among the team membership, to the detriment of its subsequent efforts.

Empowerment

Micro management is not only wasteful, but often destructive. The employees who best know how to solve a technical problem are usually first-line engineers and workers. If adequately supported, they will find all sorts of creative solutions to whatever gets in their way. Too often, managers are quick to solve problems that they only superficially understand. Such advice at best undermines the team's internal strength, and at worst misdirects them.

Empowered employees also must be kept informed of organizational strategic directions, so they can keep their project carefully synchronized with them. Traditional management has been reluctant to inform employees about corporate goals and plans, although this is changing. Not surprisingly, the Japanese tend to share their plans among all managers and among a larger fraction of their total employees than either their U.S. or European counterparts.[10] This is an expected by-product of the consensus-style interactions that typify far eastern cultures. Empowerment is probably one of the most difficult aspects of the new development paradigm for American managers, because it departs so completely from the training and cultural characteristics that have prevailed in the United States.

The leader of an empowered team plays a critical role. He or she should be a spark plug—someone who believes strongly in the development effort and will stop at almost nothing to realize it. The ideal team leader should be skilled at working with others and upbeat about resolving the many tactical issues that will surface.

The selection of the team leader is a delicate subject. On the one hand, the spirit of empowerment would suggest that the team decide its own leader, and this is often done; but, on the other hand, management might wish to assign someone who has shown from previous experience that he or she is willing and able to go the extra mile to get the job done. Some of the important factors in determining the best approach in selecting the team leader are the expected duration and complexity of the project, the experience of the work team, the extent to which the organization is familiar with empowered work teams, and the expected impact of the project on the organization. The most important factor is how much the candidate leader wants to handle the responsibility.

Although it is natural to think of the work team as an employee team, all efforts should be made to include one or more potential customers on the team. This is not always easy, since some customers wish to remain at arms-length to

---

[10]*Electronic Business*, October 7, 1991, p. 98.

their supplier community. However, enlightened customers realize that working closely with suppliers is advantageous to everyone, and they are becoming more willing to do so. However, the nature of the participation for potential customers will be different than that for employees, and the involvement will have to be adjusted according to the comfort level of the customer. Several of the following methods may be helpful to involve potential customers on the work team:

- Phone or written surveys clarifying the customer's major requirements and preferences.

- Focus groups with several customers to discuss joint market needs.

- Establishment of a single contact within the customer's organization, who is willing to be available from time to time for counsel.

- Establishment of an alliance or teaming relationship with one or more customers to share insights and mutual assistance.

- Customer evaluation of early product prototypes.

The particular approach must vary with the wishes of the customer and the nature of the project, but close involvement of some kind is critically important.

Training

A team can only be as good as its members; unfortunately, most employees have received little training in the skill set needed to implement empowered work teams. In the initial stage of team formation, there should be an understanding among the members of what is expected of them from management and from each other. Since team interactions may be new to some (or even most) members, it is strongly recommended that work teams begin their project assignment with training in related subjects. These will vary depending on the nature of the project and the expertise of the team members, but many of the subjects listed in Table 3.4 would be appropriate for product and technology development teams.

Intensive training in these areas is not practical in a short time, and such material should be incorporated into a company education program for the general population. However, the first five topics in Table 3.5 should receive immediate attention, for they specifically address the skills and tools needed to implement empowered work teams. It

TABLE 3.4. Typical subjects for team training.

	Every-one	Design	Manu-facturing	Quality	Market-ing and sales
Team relationships and interactions	X				
Problem-solving techniques	X				
The development process	X				
Principles of concurrent engineering	X				
Total quality management (TQM)	X				
QFD methodology	X				
Design for manufacturing (DFM)	X	X			
Design of experiments (DoX)		X	X	X	
Taguchi statistical techniques			X	X	
Statistical process control (SPC)			X	X	
Market launch techniques					X

would certainly be useful for a newly formed team to take a course in one or more of these subjects together as the initial aspect of their work assignment. This would not only sharpen their skills in these areas, but also help them learn to work together and trust each other.

Because of the need for immediate training by a considerable portion of a company's work force, it makes sense to solicit outside assistance from educators. Consultants may be needed in the early stages, but shortly thereafter, it is desirable to implement a cooperative arrangement with local educators (often from vocational schools and community colleges). This serves a double purpose—not only does such an arrangement train employees, it also builds competency in this area within the educational institutions, and strengthens the bonds between the universities and the company.

Collaboration between universities and industry is imperative for continued U.S. technology leadership. This is covered more extensively in chapters 11 and 12.

Management support

In the era of work teams, management's major responsibilities fall into four general areas:

- *Developing strategic product and technical directions that mesh the company's strengths with market opportunities.* With empowered work teams, a manager must provide high-value strategic leadership. The manager's responsibility is to shape the mission for the organization and make the necessary strategic and organizational decisions that guide it. Management's foremost opportunity is to establish a useful strategic planning process that most organizations woefully lack.

- *Forming and empowering appropriate work teams and providing a clear mission and goal for them.* This needn't be by decree; the best plans are usually those that percolate through the work force (especially those in contact with customers). However, it is clearly management's responsibility to determine the directions (including the boundary conditions) for the organization, guide the establishment of the appropriate work teams, and communicate their goal and objectives.

- *Supporting the team within the company infrastructure.* A manager becomes a facilitator and a motivational coach. Management training may be needed to foster these kinds of leadership skills.[11] A related responsibility is supplying the resources needed to get the job done. Without adequate resources, whether they be people, equipment, or time, a plan is merely a wish. Far too often in the era of restructuring and downsizing, so-called plans are approved with a clear recognition that the identified resources are inadequate. This is usually done in the spirit of "doing more with less" and in the name of "good corporate citizenship." But it's really admitting that the project is unimportant and that the consequent schedule overruns are acceptable and in fact, expected.

- *Providing recognition of a team's contributions.* This may not seem as crucial as it is. Virtually all employees want to be successful in the eyes of their peers, and there are very few motivators more effective and easier to implement than visible, top-down recognition for a job well done.

> Management is not "king" nor does it know all the answers. Fredrick Taylor is no longer in charge.

---

[11]P. A. Galagan, "How to Get Your TQM Training on Track," *Nation's Business,* p. 24–28, Oct. 1992.

Progress metrics

It is essential that quantitative means for determining progress be established and that the objective of the development activity be specified as quantitatively as possible. Otherwise, real misunderstandings develop over the expectations of the program. As self-empowered work teams become the rule, instead of the exception, employee compensation can be tied directly to the team's progress in meeting the program objectives. In such cases, metrics take on even greater importance. Metrics are discussed further in chapter 7.

Communications

It is imperative that the members of a multifunctional work team have regular and frequent contact with one another. Such contacts build trust, promote an understanding of and appreciation for each member's strengths and contributions, and generally create an espirit de corps focused on the team mission. In large companies, poor communications are probably the single largest cause of program failures or delays. Several approaches can be taken to foster close communications, the best of which is locating the team in a single area. Although employee movement can be costly, its payback is huge in avoiding team misunderstandings and creating an atmosphere of cooperation.

With today's high-technology capabilities, alternate approaches are practical. Electronic-mail systems are effective, especially as more and more of the work force become comfortable with PCs or terminals and reasonably facile in their writing skills. E-mail is especially effective when team members are splintered into different geographical locations. Palm-top computers, notebooks, and laptop PCs fit with modems and remote electronic-mail software expedite communications during business travel. And video-conferencing, while relatively expensive, is less so than plane and hotel fares to remote locations for a group of employees.

> It doesn't matter how team members communi-
> cate—from face-to-face to E-Mail to tin cans on a
> string. What really counts is that they do commu-
> nicate—and often!

A second important aspect of team communications re-
lates to the transferal and sharing of technical documents,
such as design specifications, assembly drawings, supplier
material requirements, cost guidelines, milestone commitments, test procedures, manufacturing or quality sign-
offs—basically all of the details that accompany a product
or technology along its path toward completion. Although
such data can be collected as paper charts and forms, many
companies have developed computer network systems
that allow team members (and managers) to store and access such data from any company location, worldwide.
Network security techniques can be used to limit access to
especially sensitive data; however, such limitations should
generally be placed upon individuals outside the work
team. All team members should be privy to nearly all data
related to the project. Network systems such as this enhance the development process in two ways:

- They eliminate delays due to incomplete documentation. Everything is in the system for instant access by
  anyone.

- They eliminate human errors caused by transferring
  data between organizations or functions. The data is
  entered one time by its originator, and the system dis-
  tributes this information in appropriate formats for
  everyone's use.

In small companies that lack a formal proprietary
system, a PC-based network can be formed inexpen-
sively. Commercial software, such as CC:Mail, Procom, or
Winfax™ can be used to enhance group communications.

TABLE 3.5. Professional growth sequence in traditional versus team-oriented product and technology development environment.*

Traditional phase	Traditional environment	Years of experi- ence	Team- oriented phase	Team-oriented environment
Internali- zation	Focuses entirely on own assignment	1–2	Team trainee	Serves in minor roles on initial team assign- ment
Collegial support	Helps close associates	2–4	Team player	Contributes to team projects
Reactive collabo- ration	Contributes to collaborative assignments	4–7	Team leader	Leads team projects
Proactive collabo- ration	Seeks collabo- ration for synergistic benefits	5–10	Department leader	Seeks teaming opportunities for product families
Leadership	Guides and establishes strategic product and technology directions	more than 10	Company leader	Guides and establishes broad strategic product and technology directions

*The team-oriented environment more quickly inserts employees into a proactive, leadership role, as indicated by the shaded areas of the table.

In such cases, it is necessary to establish a set of standard software tools (e.g., word processor, data base, spreadsheet, presentation graphics) to facilitate use within the entire organization.

PROFESSIONAL DEVELOPMENT

The professional growth of product or technology development personnel is accelerated in a team-oriented environment, as illustrated by comparing the right- and left-hand columns of Table 3.5.

In a traditional business environment, entry-level technologists initially focus on their individual assignments, with little team involvement. Over several years, they usually come to appreciate the benefits of collaboration, forming an informal network of cooperation with associates in complementary skill areas. Such relationships often endure for many years and form the basis for effective development programs. However, progress through the traditional growth sequence in the left-hand columns of Table 3.6 depends strongly on individual personality. Since technologists by definition are often less interested in social skills than in technology, many of them are slow to develop such relationships—to their detriment as well as their organization's.

In a team-oriented culture, professional development also proceeds in several phases. However, the benefits of working together are promoted much earlier, as are the skills needed for successful team participation. Organizational leadership in the team-oriented culture is fostered early as a result of top-down empowerment and through team training programs.

IN SUMMARY

The largest single ingredient in the new product development process is the use of empowered, self-directed work teams. Gone are the hand-offs between functional departments composed entirely of designers, or test engineers, or processing developers, or marketers, or quality inspectors. Instead, the people who formerly comprised these departments are now members of development teams, involved from advanced planning through customer support. Another key team member is the major customer, whose assistance is critical to fully comprehend market requirements and product trade-offs. The overall responsibility of the work team is to develop the right product and to develop the product right!

Managers must establish the mission and the boundary conditions then fully empower their work teams to handle the operational decisions. The enlightened manager

becomes a facilitator and coach for the work teams and focuses more on strategic business directions, where his or
her experience and top-level perspective can bring important guidance to the organization.

The six essential ingredients for a successful product
development program are a clear and beneficial goal, an
empowered work team, training, management recognition,
progress metrics, and communications. Communication issues are especially difficult in large organizations, and special efforts must be made, one way or another, to eliminate
them.

Finally, the personal growth of technology and product
development professionals tends to proceed more rapidly
in team-oriented environments due to the top-down empowerment that occurs in the early years of an employee's
career and his or her continuous training in building team
relationships.

CHAPTER 4

The
Process

THE DEVELOPMENT PROCESS

It is understandable for an engineer to consider a particular project unique—with its own set of customer requirements, design alternatives, and management directions. For any individual, the personal challenges may indeed be unique. But it is imperative to realize that development is first and foremost a *process*, and one that has been traveled by others before. Project delays due to rework and misdirection occur when engineers and managers fail to take advantage of process guidelines or neglect essential interactions with customers and co-workers.

In large corporations, attempts are usually made to formalize or structure the development process to guide all employees, regardless of their development experience and abilities. The risk here is unintentionally adding unneeded steps to an already complicated process. In small companies, the approach is often informal, profiting from the close interactions typical of small work groups. The ability of such companies to move quickly is envied by corporate management, and the new product and technology process described in this book attempts to simulate small-company responsiveness in a large corporate environment.

An early study of U.S. product development was carried out by R. G. Cooper and his associates between 1985 and 1988.[1,2] They studied the development characteristics of 203 business successes and failures and established a clear correlation between successful products and a complete development process. Cooper and his colleagues found that many products lacked the most elementary business requirements. For example,

- 75 percent had no market research.
- 37 percent had no business/financial analysis before development.
- 65 percent lacked pre-commercialization business analysis.
- 32 percent had no formal market launch.

However, the successful products most often underwent a complete development process that contained the following ingredients:

- A market assessment.
- A technical assessment.
- A pre-commercialization business analysis.
- A market launch.

In other words, the successful products were carefully analyzed from a business and financial perspective before the traditional development commenced, and were formally launched near the end of their development cycle. Such elements are now being folded into the development

---

[1]R. G. Cooper, "The New Product Process: A Decision Guide for Management," *Journal of Marketing Management,* vol. 3, p. 238, Spring 1988.

[2]R. G. Cooper and E. J. Kleinschmidt, "Success Factors in Product Innovation," *Industrial Marketing Management,* vol. 16, p. 215, Aug. 1987.

process in many corporations, but the extent to which they are executed varies greatly from division to division within a company, and even from product to product within a single division. Especially in large corporations, it is essential to formalize the development process to reduce the variations in its implementation by different engineers and development teams.

In another study of 254 electronic businesses, sponsored by *Electronic Business* magazine and DuPont Electronics, only 39 percent of the respondents indicated using a formal, structured product development process. More than one-third reported having no formal process, while the remaining had partially implemented processes.[3]

This data is consistent with Cooper's conclusions, and is particularly distressing in view of the fact that the *Electronic Business* 1992 CEO study indicated that new product development, technology innovation, and time-to-market were among the six most critical factors for business competitiveness.[4]

These observations illustrate how critical product development is in the business world. However, the fact that so many companies do a poor job in business and market analysis is disconcerting. In the following sections we break the development process into its components to better understand the areas that require special attention.

TRADITIONAL PRODUCT DEVELOPMENT

The development process for a sophisticated product is complex, taking anywhere from a few months to several years to complete. For example, U.S. automobiles have traditionally been on a five-year development cycle, although this is shrinking. Military vehicles (tanks, planes, ships)

[3]"39% of Companies Use a Formal Product Development Protocol," *Electronic Business*, p. 73–76, June 1992.

[4]"CEO Report," *Electronic Business*, p. 38–90, March 30, 1992.

take even longer. Advanced semiconductor memory chips are on a 10-year development cycle, with a new generation appearing every three years.[5]

Lengthy development cycles are an understandable consequence of product complexity; but they are also impacted by the degree of concurrency and the overall effectiveness of the development process. For the past several decades, traditional product development in large companies has consisted of a series of isolated work efforts carried out with multiple transfers between specialized departments.

Such development has been led by product design personnel, who bear nearly all responsibility for determining product direction and executing the development program. When the initial design is completed, it is transferred (tossed) to manufacturing and product qualification departments, which eventually do the same to the sales organization. The entire development process is carried out as a series of design-verification loops, with frequent iterations. Planning efforts prior to design are usually superficial, as is manufacturing and sales support from the development organization. It doesn't take much imagination to visualize the result: long development cycles, cost overruns, and short-lived products.

THE NEW DEVELOPMENT MODEL

There is a better way. As discussed in the previous chapter, self-empowered work teams can use a concurrent development approach to generate better products in a shorter time. Whether the product is simple or complex, a definite set of operations must be performed to bring it to successful completion. And for efficient resource utilization, these operations must be performed in a certain logical sequence—the one indicated in Figure 4.1. A brief description

---

[5]G. Larrabee and P. Chatterjee, "DRAM Manufacturing in the '90s—Part 1: The History Lesson," p. 84–87, *Semiconductor International*, May 1991.

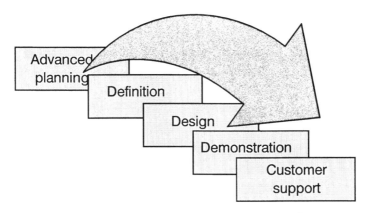

FIGURE 4.1. The five-phase product or technology development model.

of each of these five phases is provided in Table 4.1, and extensive discussions of them follow in this chapter. However, it is important to realize up-front that the phases illustrated in these charts are not really isolated or distinct but form a continuum of concurrent activities. At least—

TABLE 4.1 Major purpose of each of the five phases
in the product development process.

Phase	Purpose
Advanced planning	Planning the directions and characteristics of product families. Synchronizing product, technology, and manufacturing roadmaps.
Definition	Defining the development of a *specific product*. Matching customer needs with product benefits. Establishing resource requirements and market assessment. Preparing a business plan.
Design	Establishing all product design decisions, including its manufacture and marketing. Developing specifications for the product and its component suppliers.
Demonstration	Fabricating product prototypes. Evaluating performance against requirements. Qualifying product for production.
Customer support	Supporting the ongoing manufacturing and sales organizations to satisfy the customer's practical needs. "Whatever it takes."

that is the case for companies that have adopted the new development paradigm for their business culture.

An appreciation for each of the phases in the development process can perhaps be best described through an example that receives considerable attention in many families: the selection and construction of a house (see Table 4.2). This example is costly enough to be taken seriously

TABLE 4.2. The five-phase process illustrated for a family selecting and constructing a house.

Development phase	Typical activities
Advanced planning	Projecting family needs over 5 to 10 years: • Geographical, educational, and lifestyle preferences. • Family size considerations. • Price ranges that meet financial capabilities.
Definition	Completing plans for a specific house: • Selection of a neighborhood, housing style, and contractor that meet long- and short-term family needs. • Selection of a specific house, including the number of rooms, colors, layout, site location, landscaping options, etc. • Financial arrangements through a mortgage company.
Design	Preparing construction blueprints for the house, including site plan and list of materials and appliances.
Demonstration	Construction: • Coordination of all subcontractors. • Local building-code inspections and approvals. • Landscaping. • Purchase (closing).
Customer support	After-purchase support: • Warrantees on roof, heating, and air-conditioning. • Repair of any defects. • Possible future repair or modifications.

and is often planned more carefully than many business products. Of course, it is a product from the builder's perspective, but here, we wish to describe the process through the eyes of the customer—the family.

- The family's *advanced planning* activities are often extended over many months (if not years). What can we afford? How far from work are we willing to drive? Where are the best schools? How many bedrooms do we need? City or country living? One-floor or two-story? Advanced planning often includes drives through new neighborhoods and walks through model homes as well as the purchase of numerous home-decorating magazines to get ideas.

- During the next stage, *definition*, decisions are somehow reached on all of the various options. A contractor is selected for a particular home in a specific neighborhood. Agreement is reached on the size, shape, and layout of the house, including the stone fireplace in the bedroom, the working office at the end of the hall, and a Jacuzzi on the deck! Finances are arranged—either in the form of a construction loan or a mortgage commitment. Agreement is reached on the construction and closing schedule (which, not unlike in many business development projects, often slips!).

- During *design*, all construction details are described in a blueprint—usually with the assistance of a computer design program. This is accompanied by a detailed list of materials and sometimes specific subcontractors. A survey of the property is taken, and the exact location of the house on the site is described, including elevations and landscaping. These are still plans—but highly detailed.

- The *demonstration* phase involves all of the actual construction—digging and hammering, painting and plumbing, sheet rock and sidewalks, roofing and gutters. It is the phase that immediately comes to mind when one thinks about the process of building a house. But it is only one of five steps; it would be ridiculous to begin construction without having first carried out the previous phases with great care. We might briefly reflect on the many construction delays that occur because of poor definition activities and customer changes ("It'll cost you!").

- The *customer support* phase in this example begins with the purchase (the closing). It extends for a reasonable time after closing in order to correct any hidden defects. Usually, there are warrantees for extended periods on the roof and major appliances. And of course, the builder may become involved with the customer (buyer) again for future modifications or repair.

Each of these phases has analogous activities in the development of business projects and products. In this example, the advanced planning and definition phases are aimed at building the right house, while the final three phases focus on building the house right!

We also should indicate that the choice of five phases is somewhat arbitrary. The activities involved in the overall development process are numerous, and the division into the five phases indicated here makes most sense to the author. But one could propose that the process have only four phases (for example, by combining the first two categories into a single planning function). Even a three-phase process might be used (plan, do, support). The five phases could also be divided into very tiny increments of activities to come up with a 10- or 20-phase process. The important points are to keep the number of top-level categories relatively small, make them descriptive and simple to remember, and ensure that they contain all of the diverse elements needed to cover the two major objectives of any development program— building the right product, and building it right.

APPLICATION TO BUSINESS PRODUCT DEVELOPMENT

Of course, the simple process described above has many subelements, a few of which are illustrated in Figure 4.2. Note first that the product development process includes preparation activities for market introduction and manufacturing operations. All too often, such activities are afterthoughts in the traditional development process. Note also that the development process is not an isolated event, but one that is closely tied at both ends to ongoing business operations. Advanced planning (the first development phase) must be coupled to the company's strategic plan, while customer support (the final development phase) is integrated into the day-to-day manufacturing and sales operations. We recall from the previous chapter that the process is also

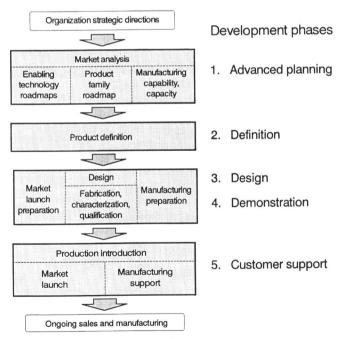

FIGURE 4.2. Conceptual flow chart of the product development cycle.
SOURCE: This chart is a simplified version, with some modifications, of a conceptual chart used by Harris Semiconductor, Melbourne, FL.

continuously linked to manufacturing, quality, R&D, sales, and marketing organizations through their representatives on the multifunctional teams that carry out the development process.

The entire development process also can be considered a product funnel, in which many possible product concepts are initially considered, only a few of which have the requisite features to undergo complete development. The process illustrated in Figure 4.3 is based on the assumption that an organization will usually have more product candidates than are worth developing from a business perspective. Because of the significant expense to develop a product, it is essential that such investment decisions are made critically.

In the sections that follow, some of the more important characteristics of each of the five development phases are described.

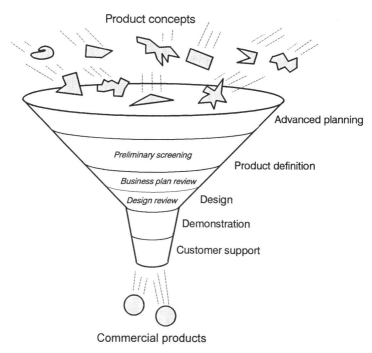

FIGURE 4.3.   The new product development funnel.

Phase 1: Advanced planning

Many large U.S. companies are in high-tech businesses. In such organizations, the business managers are most often former engineers and scientists, who know the ins and outs of their company's technology capabilities. For the most part, they enjoy interactions with their staff in such areas and tend to get caught up in the excitement about the technical features of one or another of their products. Moreover, within the spectrum of technology-rich products that have been developed by such corporations, some have been quite successful (and some have not).

It is not surprising then that product development in mature companies of this type is often pushed by technology, rather than pulled by the needs of the market (see Figure 4.4). As shown here, for the market-pull model, the product is driven by customer needs, with the challenge being to find the necessary enabling technologies to build the product. In this case, when the development is over, the products should have a buyer, since the product was

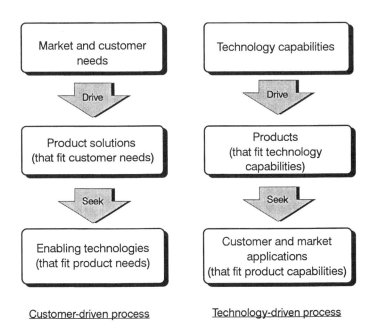

FIGURE 4.4. Customer pull versus technology push.

defined from the start in response to that customer's needs. In contrast, for the technology-driven model, the challenge is to find a customer application when the product is eventually introduced. Here, the product may or may not find eager customers, since there was no direct relationship with them in advance. Technology-push products often have too many extra features to meet price-sensitive market demands. Others may be out of step with market or customer directions and never achieve their financial expectations.

> The problem should not be finding a product for available technology, but finding a product solution to meet customer requirements.

The first objective then in advanced planning is to ensure that product development is pulled by market and customer requirements rather than pushed by whatever technology capabilities currently exist. In proceeding so, there are three major questions that the product organization must examine:

- What is the customer need?

- What is our product response to that need?

- How do we obtain the enabling technology to meet the product requirements?

As illustrated in Table 4.3, each query has several subqueries regarding the magnitude and timing of the opportunity, the nature of the product response, and the options for acquiring the enabling technology. If the product is being driven by the customer, such a series of questions will be relatively straightforward to answer. If the product is really an outcome of the company's existing technology capabilities, the answers to some will be difficult, especially in the early phases of product planning.

TABLE 4.3. The three basic questions for a customer-driven, product development organization.

What is the customer need?
- How large is the opportunity?
- How likely is it to happen?
- What is the market timing (window)?
- Is the opportunity aligned with our organizational strengths?
- What are the most important product requirements?

What is our product response to the need?
- How would we make it?
- Is our solution competitive?
- Is this good use of our product and market resources versus other opportunities?
- What are the most important enabling technology and manufacturing requirements?

Should we make or buy the required enabling technology?
- Do we have the necessary technology capabilities available?
- If not, should we develop them in-house or acquire them externally?
- Will our technology solution be cost-effective?

The tendency for American design engineers is to plunge into the development activity at a breakneck pace—presumably to get a running start on the competition, and to move into the substantial design and demonstration activities without delay. Unfortunately, such an industrious attitude, though well intentioned, is far from desirable. (Recall starting directly at the blueprint for the house construction example). Changes are expensive, and the time to make sure of the need for a new product and the form it takes is in the early stages of development.

In a classic study of military product engineering, the relative cost of several different phases of the product development cycle were compared to the impact of that phase on the total cost of the product.[6] As shown in Figure 4.5, the relative cost of the conceptual (advanced planning) phase is only 3 percent of the total product cost, yet it determines 70 percent of the total product cost throughout the life cycle of the product. In contrast, 50 percent of the product cost

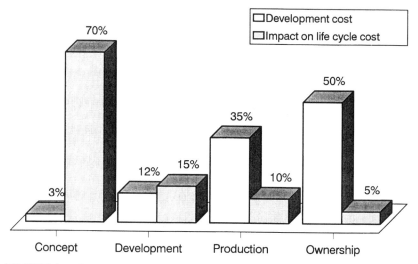

FIGURE 4.5. Relative cost of several phases of the product life cycle versus the impact of each phase on its total life cycle cost.
SOURCE: *IEEE Proceedings on Military Electronics*, August 1980.

occurs during ownership, but at that point in the product life cycle, there is no opportunity for change.

The general consensus among product development workers is that thorough up-front planning (technical, business, and marketing) is the most-overlooked activity in the product development cycle.

Advanced planning considers market directions over a period of more than five years, especially in the targeted application areas. The focus here is on a product family, which should incorporate several generations of a product under consideration as well as extensions to closely related products. Another important planning element is the expected impact of the product family on the organization's technology and manufacturing capabilities. One specific deliverable from the advanced planning phase should be the development of a product family roadmap, and its synchronization with technology and manufacturing roadmaps.

---

[6]S. G. Shina, *Concurrent Engineering and Design for Manufacture of Electronic Products*, op. cit., p. 6.

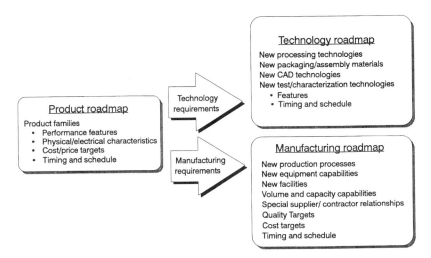

FIGURE 4.6. Synchronization of product roadmap with technology and manufacturing roadmaps.

As illustrated in Figure 4.6, the product family roadmap provides a long-range plan for the performance features and characteristics of several product generations as well as cost and price estimates for each. Most important, of course, is the schedule, which is determined by consideration of market and customer needs and the organization's capabilities to develop each product generation. Note also in Figure 4.6, that the manufacturing and technology requirements from the product roadmap drive the organization's technology and manufacturing strategic plans (i.e., roadmaps). Since each of these guides the future activities of the entire organization, a great deal of care should be given to the roadmaps, and any misalignments must be taken care of judiciously.

> "If you don't know where you are going, you will probably end up somewhere else."
> Lawrence J. Peter, *The Peter Principle*

An example of a fictitious product roadmap for a major PC supplier circa 1990 is presented in Figure 4.7. While specific capabilities and configurations are being implemented for the close-in generations (here, the 386 PCs), enabling technologies (e.g., disk drives and microprocessor chips) would be undergoing development for more distant generations, perhaps by subcontractors. For this example, the role of suppliers is especially critical, since so many of the components of a PC are standard and come from key OEM suppliers. Of course, Figure 4.7 represents only the top-level roadmap; it must be complemented with detailed technical information on all elements shown in the figure. Several features related to this roadmap should be noted:

- It must be dynamic. A product supplier must continually rethink its product family plan to ensure that it remains on target with customer needs and that it is synchronized with manufacturing and enabling technology plans. However, the basic roadmap should not be changed lightly, because of the considerable re-

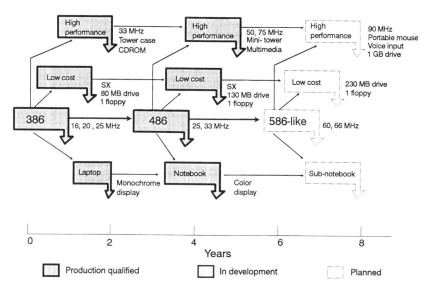

FIGURE 4.7.   Fictitious product family roadmap for a PC manufacturer, circa 1990.

source investment and lengthy lead times needed for its implementation.

- Critical (and trusted) suppliers must be knowledgeable of and committed to your roadmap. In fact, appropriate portions of your roadmap must become a part of theirs!

- The product family roadmap must be closely meshed with manufacturing and enabling technology roadmaps, as indicated. If this cannot be done during advanced planning, issues must be identified and resolved concurrently during the development process. A real danger is that roadmap inadequacies are noted, but not resolved, while the product development proceeds blindly forward. This is especially likely when the misalignments become a victim of budgetary constraints.

- The product, technology, and manufacturing roadmaps should be familiar to employees (and critical suppliers) involved in product and enabling technology development. Although some care must be taken to ensure that such information does not become accessible to competitors, it is even more important that the development teams have a keen appreciation for the major elements of these roadmaps.

- It is usually advisable to plan for an incremental family of new products. In particular, a series of modest product extensions is usually preferable to the pursuit of an infrequent home run product. Each new product within a stream of product introductions can address the most recent market changes and do so quickly enough to capture market share. In contrast, if nothing is introduced while an organization continues working on the ultimate product, a non-ending series of redesigns will be needed in response to market shifts.

In addition to the roadmaps, advanced planning should generate a top-level market and competitive analysis for the potential product family, including application areas, target market segments, potential major customers, general market requirements, and differentiating product family benefits.

Advanced planning for a single product family (as an isolated event) can be lengthy. The efficiency comes from having well understood roadmaps and analyses for major product areas, so that consideration of a new opportunity represents only an incremental effort.

Phase 2: Definition

The advanced planning phase is used to establish strategic product directions for the organization; in particular, it deals with groups or families of products. During the definition phase, the development process shifts to *individual* product candidates that are being considered within the overall product family guidelines. During definition, screening of product candidates continues in the search for the best choices, and a thorough business plan is established for those that make this screening cut. These activities proceed in a three-step sequence:

1. New product ideas and concepts are captured and screened for initial merit.
2. Product candidates that pass the initial screening based on their financial and technical merits are defined in detail against customer requirements.
3. A detailed business plan is prepared for any product that is selected to undergo the remainder of the development process.

These steps are considered individually below.

Initial screening

Obviously, the more product ideas entering the initial part of the product funnel, the better. Consequently, an organization should set up a methodology to capture potential product ideas from any source. Again, close contact with potential customers is essential, for they will probably be the source of many, if not most, of the product concepts. However, once captured, product ideas must be screened critically, so that only the best progress to the next phase of the development process.

For initial product concept screening, the candidate product is often championed by only one or two people. However, the organization should insist that any new ideas for serious consideration be reviewed with a team of experienced product leaders that is formed for just that purpose. Although brief, this preliminary screening should address product features, top-level customer and market requirements, major competitive positions, and approximate magnitude of development effort needed. As we have indicated, the level of investment increases dramatically as a product traverses the five-phase development cycle. Therefore, the major purpose of the screening is to determine whether or not the product concept merits the additional investment (typically $10,000 to $100,000) needed to define the product and prepare a business plan for it.

Product definition

This is one of the most critical (and often most poorly executed) segments of the product development cycle. Its basic objective is to optimally match product benefits and features with customer requirements. To do so, a thorough analysis must be carried out; first and foremost, customer requirements must be understood, and the product must be specified to meet them cost-effectively. Such an interaction requires detailed consideration of numerous variables, but pays off by simplifying the product and reducing its cost. A sample of typical customer and product variables is illustrated in Table 4.4. Obviously, the number of trade-off decisions is large, requiring a systematic methodology to evaluate the many alternatives. Quality function deployment (QFD) is an established methodology that can be used by the product definition team to examine trade-offs for this purpose. The QFD methodology is described further in chapter 6.

TABLE 4.4. Typical customer and product variables.

Customer variables	Product variables
Physical	• Process technology
• Size	• Assembly technology
• Weight	• Material or component selection
• Appearance	• Packaging density
— Style	• Design architecture
— Color	• Product complexity
— Shape	• Capability options
• Portability	
• Strength	
Functional	
• Performance specs	
— Speed	
— Voltage	
— RPM	
— Quietness	
— Power consumption	
• Operating range	

The need for customer participation during the definition phase of product or technology development is absolutely critical. This has been one of the greatest strengths of Japanese manufacturers in their climb to technology prominence. The mutual participation of suppliers, developers and customers in the Japanese keiretsu system is frequent and strong (recall Table 3.1 in chapter 3). Since the equivalent of keiretsus does not exist in the United States, special efforts must be made to involve major customers and suppliers. Strong customer involvement will dramatically increase the chances of a successful market introduction and help avoid unnecessary features that are not cost-effective in the eyes of the user.

> Customers really don't care about products per se, they want solutions.[7]

TABLE 4.5. Magnitude of investment
for different phases of the development process.

Phase	Number of product candidates	Number of employees per product candidate	Magnitude of investment
Advanced planning	10–100	< 1	Insignificant
Definition	5–10	2–5	$10–$100K
Design, demonstration, customer support	2–5	5–50	$500K–$10M

As indicated in Table 4.5, each step in the development process involves an increasing number of people and additional expenses. Once the product business plan has been approved, the development costs increase by 10- to 100-fold, as the product undergoes design and demonstration efforts prior to market launch and product introduction.

Business plan

The final activity during the definition phase is the preparation of a business plan, which should be reviewed by management to ensure that the product candidate meets the financial and business guidelines of the organization and that it is the best candidate among the several product investment opportunities that exist. The business plan includes resource needs and product development schedule; it forecasts revenue, costs, and payback. The schedule and resource requirements must be realistically projected. Padding and being overly optimistic are equally harmful in destroying a team's credibility—not to mention the financial impact of a distorted market entry date. The projections must be based on experience and knowledge—not on whimsy or hope. The business plan should also identify development risks, whether they be technical or market related. By con-

---

[7]H. Garrett DeYoung, "Making R&D Pay Off Better and Quicker," *Electronic Business*, December 1992, pp. 61–64.

sidering risks up front, a product strategy can often be established that successfully sidesteps some of them.

At the completion of the product definition stage, the organization must be convinced that the candidate is the right product (from a financial and business perspective), and that the proposed plan will develop the product right (see Figure 4.8). The product must make sense from all perspectives before significant investments are made in carrying out the many technical parts of the development cycle.

We should note that the extensive definition activities discussed here cannot help but increase the time spent during this phase of the development process. However, as a result of the additional planning and definition efforts, considerable reductions can usually be made in the demonstration phase, where traditional delays and redesigns are more the norm than the exception. This is illustrated graphically in Figure 4.9.

Phase 3: Design

In this phase, the technical product design is completed, including consideration of all physical, electrical, mechan-

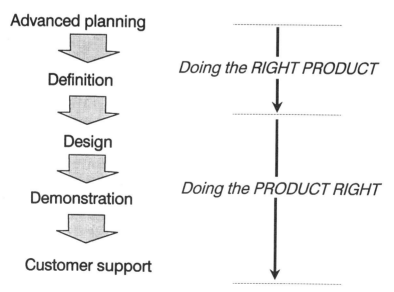

FIGURE 4.8.   Doing the right product and doing the product right.

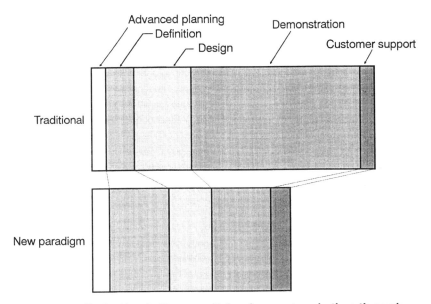

FIGURE 4.9. Reduction in the overall development cycle time through more extensive front-end planning and definition activities.

ical, and thermal interactions. Equally important, the detailed plans for manufacturing and marketing are completed. A brief summary of some of the major elements in each of these areas is presented in Table 4.6, and discussed further below.

TABLE 4.6. Product design elements.

Technical design	Manufacturing preparation	Marketing/sales preparation
• Product schematic	• Process flow	• Beta site
• Component layout	• Assembly flow	arrangements
• Material	• Yield projections	• Advertising
specifications	• Quality assurance	• Sales promotion
• Computer	tests	• Product
simulations	• Volume and	announcements
• Test plan	capacity plan	• Inventory
• Supply partner		• Distribution network
arrangements		
• Patent and copyright		
plans		

The major design issues are established by the broad participation of most of the work team, including customers, designers, and assembly and test personnel. Reducing the unit production cost is usually a critical team objective, and design alternatives are vigorously pursued to that purpose. Early identification of problems is essential, since only with such identification can their resolution be addressed.

In the technical area, computer models are used more and more often to assist design teams and reduce the extent of prototype testing. Such is the case, for example, in the following development areas:

- Electrical layouts and simulations for IC chips and printed circuit boards.
- 3-D physical design layouts.
- Simulated stress analysis of mechanical structures (for weak spots).
- Wind velocity simulation of auto, plane, and missile prototypes.
- Wiring diagrams of complex electronic systems.

The critical parameters, boundary conditions, and key results of such models, layouts, and simulations should be thoroughly documented during the design phase and included in the design review that serves as the gate for the next step in the development process.

The strength of multifunctional work teams is the breadth of their experience in virtually all relevant technical and business areas. During the design phase, plans are completed for virtually every detail that can be anticipated in advance.

The key ingredient for an effective design effort is anticipation. Most development delays are caused not by unusual problems but by unanticipated ones.

As long as a potential problem can be anticipated, it generally can be resolved. This reduces the chance that re-designs—with their deleterious impact on development cycle time—will be needed.

Such anticipation extends in a technical sense even to the intricacies of the product design itself. With considerable effort, an organization can develop a set of tools and a methodology to design products that take into account the limits of the manufacturing or assembly processes. Called design for manufacturing (DFM) or design for assembly (DFA), such techniques statistically determine the magnitude of the manufacturing and assembly variations and build appropriate limits into the product design tools. Similar limits can be applied to testing variations (design for test). Testing is becoming an increasingly important factor in product development, because of the increasing complexity of the product design and the emergence of self-diagnostic computer-automated testing.

The effectiveness of the concurrent design process and the focus on design simplification is evident in all sorts of modern products: snap-together plastic parts that replace screws and bolts; electronic controllers that eliminate mechanical gearing and pneumatic drive systems; and one-piece, molded plastic that replaces several components constructed of various materials. The increasing electronic content in automobiles reflects the elimination of mechanical parts as well as the incorporation of multiple electrical components into electronic modules (with further reductions in part counts). In Figure 4.10, the parts needed to manufacture a thermal viewer for a military tank are illustrated before and after a design effort was initiated by the developer, Hughes Aircraft, with a focus on design for manufacturing and design for assembly.[8] The final product had only a third as many parts as the earlier version and yielded a production cost 74 percent lower!

---

[8]"Designing Reality," *Vectors* Vol. 35, No. 2 (Los Angeles: Hughes Aircraft, 1993), pp. 6–9.

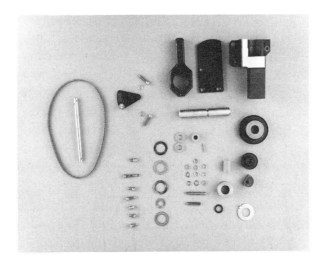

FIGURE 4.10. Parts that comprise a Driver's Thermal Viewer for a military tank, before and after a Hughes Aircraft design team focus on design for manufacturing and design for assembly.
SOURCE: Photos provided courtesy of Hughes Aircraft Company.

Manufacturing and marketing plans must also be completed during the design phase, as already indicated in Table 4.6. The manufacturing organization must have the details worked out for the specific processes that will be used as well as any additional equipment needed for the expected volumes. Similarly, a quality assurance plan to test the product to its specified limits must be established, including the number and precise configuration of the samples. Finally, forecast manufacturing and test yields must be reexamined to calculate the expected product costs. Because of the constant downward pressure on selling price, the product design must be acutely sensitive to manufacturing and test yields.

Marketing and sales organizations can get a running start on the forthcoming product introduction by completing all their plans for advertising and product promotion. Artwork, slogans, and marketing messages must be developed as well as commitments to trade journals. Exhibits at trade shows take considerable advance preparation, as do the commitments to participate. Too many activities like this are considered at the last minute, with ineffective results. A common flaw in product development activities regards advertising and marketing budgets. Traditional practice often has advertising responsibilities (and budgets) separate from product development, resulting in a dogfight for funds when they are needed (usually very late in the development process). The modest cost of advertising should be considered up-front and included in the overall budget for the product development effort. With the considerable cost of product development, there is no legitimate excuse for marketing not to be completely in step with the technical development activities. During the design phase, the plans for the advertising and marketing campaign should be completed and reviewed as part of the overall product design activity.

At the completion of the design phase, a management review (traditionally called a design review) is held, during which a decision must be made regarding continuation or redirection of the development. At this formal review, all aspects of the design phase should have been completed— the design of the product and detailed plans for its manufacturing and sale.

Phase 4: Demonstration

This is the "do" phase. For product development, prototypes should be processed in modest quantities to allow statistically valid evaluation over the necessary operational ranges (e.g., temperature, cycles of operation). Test programs should be completed and used for the final evaluation of packaged units. Sufficient quantities of the product must be prepared to support not only functional evaluation but also formal product qualification tests. As soon as appropriate, samples should be provided to selected major customers for their initial evaluation and feedback. And very important, market launch material should be in the final stages of preparation for full-blown product introduction.

In manufacturing, product yield data should be gathered and analyzed to begin optimization. Special attention should be paid to sample lots that have especially low or high yields to identify the critical variables. Final product specifications should be determined to support sales and advertising literature. And the formal product qualification tests should be completed and documented.

As a result of the extensive planning that preceded it, the demonstration phase should go smoothly, certainly much more so than it would otherwise have done without the extensive definition and design activities. Barriers should have been eliminated in advance, and computer simulations carried out for the design review should allow first-time prototyping success, or close to it. If revisions are required, either of two paths must be followed, as illustrated schematically in Figure 4.11:

- If the original approach is sound but additional data is needed, or if a design tweak is required, an incremental loop takes the development team back to the design phase, where technical revisions are made. This will delay the schedule by several weeks, which represents a moderately severe penalty in the quest for rapid time-to-market. The schedule for marketing and man-

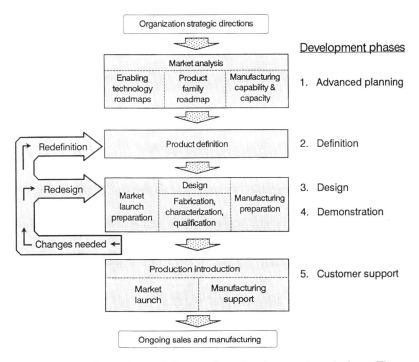

FIGURE 4.11. Flow chart of the product development cycle from Figure 4.2 with a design iteration.

ufacturing plans will have to be adjusted as a result of such action.

- However, if the basic approach is found lacking, or the product is unable to meet its original objectives, the process must be reset back to the definition phase. Such a delay can cripple the momentum of the product team, and perhaps alter the project irreversibly.

Additional cycles and delays such as these illustrate why the design and demonstration phases must be executed so thoroughly.

> Rapid development cycles require first-time success. Period.

Phase 5: Customer support

This final stage of development involves the transition from product development to manufacturing and marketing and sales. Therefore, it includes manufacturing in the standard production facility at acceptable yields and in sufficient quantities to meet initial inventory levels and customer samples. It also includes market introduction, or launch, shortly thereafter.

Manufacturing transfer

In traditional product development, this was often the final responsibility of the product development team, with a ceremonial sign-off and transfer to a new team (manufacturing). The following inadequacies are only a slight exaggeration:

- The product development personnel usually went to new assignments and helped resolve subsequent manufacturing difficulties primarily as personal favors.

- The product design was insensitive to manufacturing process variations. It pushed the envelope of several processing variables.

- Because of all sorts of day-to-day pressures, manufacturing had to scramble to incorporate the new product into the appropriate process.

- Product volume estimates were patently unbelievable.

- Necessary processing or testing equipment from third-party suppliers was late in arriving.

- Quality testing was not considered adequately in advance—special product configurations or procedures were not ready on time.

It just didn't get much worse!

Production personnel will struggle unnecessarily with process and test issues if their involvement with the development team throughout the earlier stages has been limited. Conversely, if manufacturing and marketing organizations have participated as members of the work team throughout the development phases, most issues will have been anticipated, and the final production and operations support stage will be more nearly routine.

Market introduction

In some businesses, such as entertainment, popular literature, and autos, product launch takes on monumental importance. In the entertainment field, not a night goes by when a TV talk-show host isn't helping a guest promote his fall TV series or her Broadway opening. Boxing matches, dubbed the "The Final Battle" and the like are advertised weeks in advance to boost pay-for-view sales. And billboards and bus posters are bedecked with the latest soft drink product. But technical products outside of the glittery sports or entertainment industries are usually promoted more discretely—reflecting in part their target customers, the modest size of their advertising budget, and unfortunately, the typical disinterest in marketing by the engineering and technical communities that create such products. Although it may not be appropriate to announce the market introduction of a new type of bicycle seat on the Letterman show, it is equally ridiculous to simply have it show up one day on the shelf of a few retail stores.

At this point in the development process, the market introduction should be briskly occurring—the planning for it having been completed for the design review. Activities such as the following should be woven into the market introduction:

- Training information for the sales team.
- Promotional events at trade shows.

- Advertising in trade literature.

- Direct mailing to focused customer prospects.

- Technical seminars for potential customers.

- Press releases sent to selected trade journals.

- Buttons worn by employees.

Most important are the continuing and growing contacts with the potential major customers that have participated to some extent as team members in the development process.

In all of these activities, the product message should be on customer benefits—not product features (remember the market pull!). Recall the bored Maytag repairman. His company's product message for years has been reliability—not technical information about dishwashers or clothes dryers.

For any type of development, there is an important element of customer satisfaction. If the development is a product, the customer is external—if the development is enabling technology or applied research, the customer is a manufacturing or engineering organization. In all cases, the goal is nothing short of a satisfied customer, and the development team's job is not complete until that goal is obtained.

Finally, the various elements of the new development paradigm are indicated in Figure 4.12 in a manner that shows where each has the greatest impact in the five stages of product development. Immediately apparent is the planning impact provided by the vision statement, the product and technology roadmaps, and customer participation (doing the right things). In contrast, the use of multifunctional work teams, metrics, concurrent development, and DFM or DFT encompass the entire development cycle, with emphasis on doing things right. The obvious conclusion from this chart is that the development process must incorporate most of the elements described above to expect to favorably impact the overall development cycle.

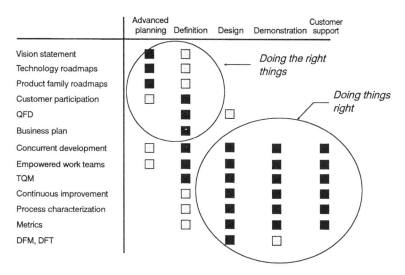

FIGURE 4.12. New development activities and their occurrence throughout the five phases of development.
(Dark squares denote a strong impact, while the shaded squares denote a secondary effect.)

WARNING #1—FOCUS

One problem in the implementation of any development process is spreading development resources too thin. Regarding human resources, it is much in vogue for professionals to be perceived as workaholics, making themselves exceptionally busy through involvement in more activities than they can effectively handle. The current lean organization, with large management span of control and engineering resources stretched to the limit encourages such behavior. When contributors take on too many responsibilities to the point at which each activity must wait for attention, the development cycle time becomes the victim. Everything takes forever to complete. For example, if a designer is simultaneously juggling numerous product designs, their completion time depends on the number of designs being handled as well as on his or her design completion rate (in a non-shared mode). That is:

$$\text{Design cycle time} = \frac{\text{Number of active design jobs}}{\text{Design completion rate}}$$

To be specific, if a designer is simultaneously designing five products, and his or her design rate is typically four months per design, none of the projects is likely to be completed before 20 months (see Figure 4.13).

> Being partly done with many projects translates to being late to the market with all!

Clearly, the market impact of this designer's products would be much greater if he or she completed one design before accepting responsibility for the next. Similar queing delays can occur throughout many of the activities in the development process.

It is better to focus on one project and complete it quickly than to move forward (slowly) with many projects at the same time. And yet the latter option is the norm in most technical organizations today.

A second problem with multiplexing responsibilities lies in the fact that efforts usually are applied disproportionately

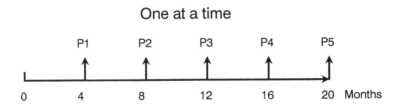

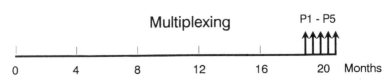

FIGURE 4.13.   Multiplexing five products versus completing each in sequence.

to the easiest of a group of projects. At any given time, some tasks progress smoothly, while others struggle—allowing little progress despite moderate efforts (see Figure 4.14). In such a scenario, it is natural to focus on the easier task, postponing efforts on the one that is stuck. After all, the first brings peer admiration, management compliments, and personal gratification, while the lack of progress on the second may not cause personal problems for a while. However, the importance of a project is usually unrelated to the barriers that are presented—in fact, if anything, the more difficult job usually brings with it the greatest impact. Consequently, a second danger with multiplexing is that important jobs may be delayed at the expense of easier, less important ones.

Wherever appropriate, it is valuable to assign an individual to only one major activity. Specifically, the leader and critical members of a work team should be devoted to a single project.

The benefits of a focused activity are especially apparent if incremental resources can be made available for a single specific task. Hiring a consultant or a retired former employee to work exclusively on a single project will

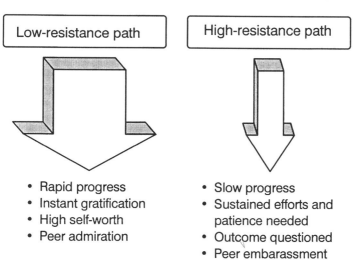

Low-resistance path	High-resistance path
• Rapid progress • Instant gratification • High self-worth • Peer admiration	• Slow progress • Sustained efforts and patience needed • Outcome questioned • Peer embarassment

FIGURE 4.14. Rewards and benefits that accompany efforts on low-resistance, rapid-progress activities versus slow-moving, high-resistance projects.

dramatically accelerate that task compared to the slow rate of progress that would occur if the same task were assigned to the back burner of a regular employee. With more and more right-sizing and outsourcing, experienced professionals may be readily available for just such focus.

WARNING #2—TERMINATE LOSERS

We have shown how the cost of product or technology development continues to increase as the product passes through each of the phases of the development process. We have also shown the impact on development cycle time when critical team members are stretched too thin. For each of these reasons it is essential for managers to terminate or redirect programs just as soon as it becomes apparent that the original project goals cannot be reasonably achieved.

In traditional corporate engineering and product development organizations, it seems to be extremely difficult to terminate a project. There are several reasons for this:

- The people involved in the project do not wish to admit (even to themselves) that they are unable to meet the objectives. There is always one more thing to try!
- Termination is not really considered an option. Regardless of the difficulties and redirections the project has faced, the reasons that were once given for the value of the product are assumed to remain valid.
- The initial objectives are forgotten or distorted in the midst of a series of technical issues and their ensuing solutions.
- Engineers become emotionally involved with the technical challenges, and continue bootlegging project activities long after management believes that work has been terminated.

It is the responsibility of the work team to alert management to problems that are not being effectively resolved, and it is the responsibility of management to kill (or redirect) a project that is unlikely to meet its original objectives.

IN SUMMARY

Studies by Cooper in the late '80s showed that for successful products, market and technical assessments were done before engineering development and a formal market launch was conducted to initiate market penetration. Despite the importance of these attributes, other studies show that few products include such a complete development program.

The most important part of this chapter addresses the fact that development is a *process*—one that is carried out repeatedly by many different people and teams throughout a large organization. Hence, the specifics of this process must be well understood and optimized.

The product development process can be conveniently broken into five major phases. The first two phases are planning functions: Advanced planning deals with a family of products and their long-term enabling technology and manufacturing capabilities, while definition deals with the specific product of immediate interest. During definition, the business and financial merits of the product are accessed before significant investments are made in the technical portion of the development program. Customer requirements are also considered carefully in determining the features that are incorporated into the product. In the third phase, design, the technical approach is established, taking into consideration manufacturing and sales issues, while in the demonstration phase, prototypes are prepared and their performance is evaluated against expectations. In the last phase, customer support, the development team assists the manufacturing and sales organizations to satisfy practical customer requirements—in whatever form they may take. A market launch is the culmination of marketing efforts that have been shaped throughout a substantial portion of the development process. Finally, the activities required in each of these phases must occur concurrently to the greatest extent possible.

Throughout the development process, resources must be sufficiently focused to meet requirements. Well-intentioned, ambitious engineers who multiplex several assignments simultaneously usually add unnecessary delays to each of them. Finally, it is essential that the work teams and their management leaders consider product termination as a realistic option when the project runs into serious complications.

In chapters 5 and 11, we will show that the five-phase process discussed here is quite generic and can be applied to product development, enabling technology development, and even applied research programs.

CHAPTER 5

Research
and Technology
Development

ENABLING TECHNOLOGIES

Large corporations typically introduce hundreds of new products each year—a few of which represent major innovative advancements, and many of which are modest (but valuable) extensions of products that already exist. Both types of products are usually based on a foundation of enabling technologies—that is, software tools for design and component layout, a set of manufacturing processes to fabricate components and modules, and packaging or assembly technologies to shape the product into its final configuration. The following are examples of enabling process technologies:

- Photographic developing and printing.
- Commercial wine making.
- Pharmaceutical manufacturing processes.
- Commercial baking for bread, doughnuts, and cookies.
- Cereal packaging.
- Metal refining.

- Leather tanning and curing.
- Milk pasteurization.
- Mining, extracting quarry stone.

Typically, technologies such as these are designed to serve several families of products, thereby leveraging the manufacturer's investment in technology development. Compared to development of an individual product, enabling technology development programs generally have:

- Longer completion times.
- Higher costs.
- Broader specifications.
- Greater risk.

For example, development of the technologies to support the next generation of an advanced integrated circuit may take four to five years, involve scores of engineers, and cost tens of millions of dollars.[1] In contrast, the development of a single product, once all of the enabling technologies are in place, usually occurs in a fraction of that time and at correspondingly less cost. However, longer schedules and broader specifications should not permit technology development to be managed more casually than the development of a specific product. Often such programs are driven by technologists with little knowledge of (or sensitivity to) customer and market needs. Although this may have been standard operating procedure in the '60s and '70s, it is unacceptable in the current era of scarce resources and intense global competition. In fact, one can argue that the lengthy schedules and higher costs associated with enabling technology development demand a greater management focus to ensure successful and timely project completion.

---

[1]G. Larrabee and P. Chatterjee, *Semiconductor International,* p. 84–87, May 1991.

Admittedly, there can be a considerable element of uncertainty in technology development. However, with the close collaboration of customer and technologist, the unknown variables and the time required to resolve technical issues usually can be managed. Most technology approaches have alternatives, and collaboration can often provide at least one workable path within the required opportunity window. What is no longer acceptable is a hands-off attitude for technology development—one typified by the following expressions (and the response of customers):

- "We'll let you know when we've got it" (How about working together on it?).

- "We're planning some really interesting experiments" (We'd prefer relevant).

- "It may take another year or so" (Let's look at some alternatives).

In chapters 3 and 4, we discussed the attributes of the new product development process, including a description of its five phases. The major elements of the new product development paradigm were found to be:

- Empowered, multifunctional work teams.

- Customer and supplier participation.

- Product benefits matched to customer requirements.

- Extensive up-front planning.

- Concurrent development.

- Product roadmaps linked to manufacturing and enabling technology roadmaps.

- Managers focused on strategic issues and team facilitation.

In this chapter, we will show that the same product development process, including the attributes listed above, are directly extendible to enabling technology development and even to applied research. As an example, in Table 5.1, we illustrate the considerable similarities in the five major development phases for product and enabling technologies. Although this is a detailed chart, it shows that for process technology, packaging technology, and CAD system technology, virtually every activity in the product development sequence has an analogous activity in enabling technology development. This should come as no surprise, since the five-step product development process described in earlier sections defines a near-universal sequence: plan, define, design, demonstrate, support.

What is perhaps worth emphasizing is that technology development can and should be managed as a product. It has customers and deliverables, boundary conditions, time restraints, resource limitations, and opportunity windows— all the attributes of a product. And the need for careful advanced planning, program definition, teamwork, and customer support is every bit as important in applied research and enabling technology development programs as it is in conventional product development. In simple terms, both products and technology development must pass through the same five-phase process. The specifics may differ, but the sequence and basic approach are the same.

The following activities within the five-phase development process are common to both products and technologies:

- *Roadmaps.* All enabling technologies should have extended 5-year plus roadmaps that are synchronized with their product family and manufacturing counterparts. These are developed in the advanced planning phase.

- *Customer requirements and expected benefits.* During the definition phase, these must be carefully matched for

TABLE 5.1. Elements comprising the five stages of product development and enabling technology development.

Stage	Product development	Enabling Process development	Technology Assembly development	Development CAD system development
Advanced planning	• Product family roadmaps • Market applications	• Processing roadmaps • Product applications	• Packaging roadmaps • Product applications	• CAD system roadmaps • Product applications
Definition	• Customer requirements • Product benefits • Product specifications • Schedule and re-source requirements • Business plan	• Customer requirements • Process benefits • Process specifications • Schedule and resource requirements • Financial impact analysis	• Customer requirements • Packaging technology benefits • Package specifications • Schedule and resource requirements • Financial impact analysis	• Customer requirements • CAD system benefits • CAD system specs • Schedule and resource requirements • Financial impact analysis
Design	• Product design • Product test plan • Product qualification plan • Market introduction plan	• Process design • Process test plan • Process qualification plan • Manufacturing introduction plan	• Package design • Package test plan • Package qualification plan • Manufacturing introduction plan	• CAD system design • CAD system test plan • CAD system qualification plan • Beta site plan
Demon-stration	• Product prototypes • Product characterization • Product qualification	• Process test vehicles • Process characterization • Process qualification	• Package prototypes • Package characterization • Package qualification	• Program code • System characterization • System qualification
Customer support	• Production introduction • Manufacturing yield enhancement • Market introduction	• Manufacturing introduction • Line yield enhancement • Initial product support	• Manufacturing introduction • Line yield enhancement • Initial product support	• Engineering introduction • Design bug elimination • Initial product support

any development effort requiring the allocation of resources (dollars, facilities, or people). An understanding of the customers' needs is always required.

- *Schedule.* The need for careful planning and tracking of enabling technologies is especially critical, since delays in technology development can ripple down, causing a corresponding slippage in the introduction of the various products that may be based on it.

- *Customer focus.* Technology transfer is enhanced if the end user is regarded as a paying customer (which is the case). Even though the enabling technology development customer may be the product or engineering organization in the same company, internal customers must be taken just as seriously and be satisfied just as completely as external ones.

- A development program is not completed until the product or technology is running smoothly (yielding!). For product development, manufacturing focus is on product yield; for process-related technology development, process or assembly line yields are more relevant. For software development, eliminating bugs in the program code is equivalent to increasing the yield of manufacturing technologies.

One difference between the two types of development is the financial analysis that is required during the definition phase. For product development, a complete business plan is needed, including competitive and market analysis, forecast revenues and costs. For technology development, such an analysis can be impractical because of the wide range of products supported by a single technology (e.g., packaging). However, an estimate of expected product families, sales volumes, and required product manufacturing costs should be reviewed to ensure a reasonable payback against expected investment. Sufficient consideration should also be given to make-buy options for acquiring enabling technology capabilities.

RESEARCH AND DEVELOPMENT

It is reasonable to determine what kinds of R&D might not follow the process described in this book. To answer that, we turn to the definition of basic research, applied research, and development presented in Table 5.2. These definitions come primarily from the National Science Foundation, which sponsors a considerable amount of university R&D. From these definitions, there appear to be two factors that impact the applicability of our five-phase process:

TABLE 5.2. Definition of basic research, applied research, and development.

Basic research:	The study of phenomena purely for the purpose of gaining more complete knowledge or understanding of the subject under study, without specific applications in mind.* It is sometimes called pure research because it is uncontaminated by profit motives.**
Applied research:	The investigation of technologies to determine the means by which a specific, recognized need may be met. It includes studies to discover new knowledge with commercial applicability to products, processes, or services.
Development:	The systematic application of advanced knowledge or technology toward the production of useful materials, devices, systems, or methods, including the design of prototypes and processes. Exploits new technologies to design products that are practical, reliable, and manufacturable.

*This definition is similar, but not identical, to that used by the National Science Foundation for its research surveys.

**This part of the definition is taken from L. Geppert, "Industrial R&D: the New Priorities," *IEEE Spectrum*, p. 34, Sept. 1994.

1. The degree of discovery that is needed to reach the objectives. A considerable need for discovery would make advanced planning of the entire project very difficult.

2. The objective of the work with respect to addressing an end-user (customer) need.

For development projects, customer needs are well defined, and the expectation of scientific or technological discovery is relatively small. Hence, the five-phase process is clearly relevant to development projects.

For applied research projects, the potential applications (customer requirements) are usually reasonably well defined, and a scientific approach, though far from certain, is usually sufficient to allow the preparation of a plan. In fact, most applied research programs that are funded by the federal government require a detailed approach and objectives in the formal proposal for consideration of award. Hence, although the element of discovery exists, it is usually insufficient to prevent the kind of planning and definition functions described throughout the previous chapter.

Basic research is probably the single exception to the generic process described in chapter 4. Here, the need for discovery is great, making a schedule of expected progress difficult. In addition, the applicability of the work to a specific customer or group of customers may not always be possible. Hence, thorough up-front definition and customer support are not applicable. In addition, metrics related to progress are usually based on time lines of one kind or another, and these too are difficult to establish for basic research.

However, we should hasten to add that many parts of the development process still are relevant—even for basic research. In particular, most basic research should have an ultimate end user in mind, even if the end user is another scientist who will take the results of the research and extend them further. Close collaboration of the researcher and the end user would still be valuable for the overall success of the research.

IN SUMMARY

Enabling technology is a term used to describe the various physical and chemical processes, CAD systems, and packaging and assembly processes that are used as a foundation in the development of a family of specific products. The development of such technologies can and should be treated like the development of a product. Its customers should be strongly participative and must be satisfied; it should be planned and defined thoroughly to develop the right technology; it should be carried forward by multifunctional engineering teams; and it should be managed (and monitored) intensely so that the technology is done right. For the most part, the five-phase development model for product development is extendible to enabling technology development.

In considering research, we conclude that applied research—like development—can be effectively described by the processes, methodologies, and metrics described throughout this book. However, basic research, which has no definitive applications and considerable need for discovery, is generally not able to be simulated with our process model. Although the five-phase process described in this volume does have very broad technical applicability, it does rely on the need for strong customer participation and realistically scheduled project activities.

CHAPTER 6

The Tools

and Methods

In preceding chapters we discussed two complementary aspects of the new development paradigm: the people and the process. In this chapter, we describe some of the most effective tools and methods used to implement the new approaches. Topics such as total quality management (TQM), concurrent engineering, and reengineering can be regarded as quality programs, but their applicability to product and technology development underscores their universal effectiveness. Other topics such as quality function deployment (QFD), technology transfer, design re-use, and innovation are more specific to our development focus. Both types of tools and methods should be able to find an important place in the reader's development arsenal.

GENERAL QUALITY METHODS

Total quality management (TQM)

This activity embraces the philosophy of continuous improvement—never accepting business as usual. It's not just product or technology development, but how a company handles deliveries, takes orders, receives phone calls—everything. As such, it is sufficiently universal to include concurrent development, self-directed work teams, and gain-sharing. However, in practice, it usually focuses on three elements:

- Customer satisfaction.

- Continuous improvement.

- Process emphasis.

TQM primarily helps do the job right. Its focus on customer satisfaction guides an organization toward activities that have a short-term practical impact—whether they involve products (for external customers) or enabling technology (for internal customers). Its focus is largely incremental—exploring ways of doing things more efficiently today than yesterday.

Some of the differences in carrying out day-to-day business practices with a TQM attitude are illustrated in Table 6.1. The tenets of customer satisfaction and continuous improvement are obvious throughout this table.

For example, Motorola is one of many companies that has made impressive business strides through TQM. In 1988, it launched its now-famous Six-Sigma program to reduce component defect levels to below 3.4 per million. In this program, Motorola requires each of its employees to spend 40 hours of quality training annually, for which it spends 3.2 percent of its total payroll. It also created Motorola University for quality-oriented employee training, and won the 1988 Malcolm Baldrige National Quality Award. Most important, the $11B company claims to have cut costs by $2.7B annually.[1]

The impact of TQM on defect levels in electronics companies over the past five years is shown in Figure 6-1. Interestingly, these companies report that the major quality gains have come from their component suppliers. None-

---

[1] "TQM Reality Check: It Works, but It's Not Cheap or Easy," *Electronic Business,* Oct. 1992, p. 50.

TABLE 6.1. TQM versus traditional business attitudes.

Traditional attitudes	Total quality management attitudes
• If it ain't broke, don't fix it.	• Fix it anyway!
• Quality comes through rigorous inspection procedures to eliminate defects.	• Quality is built in.
• Customers are outsiders.	• Customers are critical and vital components of our organization.
• Quality is defined by our quality control department.	• The customer defines quality for us.
• It is wasteful to spend too much time on an unimportant job.	• Every job deserves a 100 percent effort.
• Supplier relationships are necessarily adversarial due to pricing negotiations.	• Suppliers, especially critical ones, are members of our work teams. They should be considered our partners.
• Quality improvement is costly.	• Quality improvement reduces costs and saves money.
• Quality improvement is primarily a management issue.	• Quality is everyone's job.

theless, the overall impact of suppliers plus in-house activities is a 17 percent to 39 percent defect reduction in each of the past five years.

The single shortcoming of TQM is its incremental focus. Keep in mind, most of what is being done today will also be important tomorrow, and most short-term customer-oriented needs are critical to an operation's ongoing business success. However, some portion of an organization, particularly in the area of product and technology development, must be sensitive to future needs that are unrecognized by the customer and to revolutionary solutions that may make today's incremental improvements obsolete.

Some of the programs that fall under the TQM umbrella but that are directly applicable to product and technology development, are described in the following sections.

Percent defect reduction

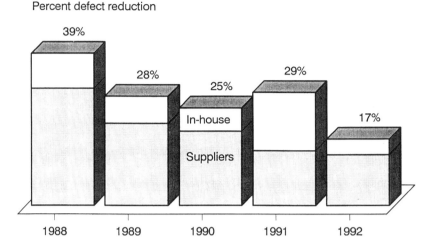

FIGURE 6.1. **Effects of TQM programs on defect reduction in the U.S. electronics industry.**
SOURCE: American Electronics Association 1992 productivity study conducted by Pittiglio, Rabin, Todd, and McGrath and KPMG Peat Marwick.

Customer satisfaction

Many companies are now developing formal statistical approaches for monitoring their customers' degree of satisfaction with their products. One technique, called gap analysis, has been described by Harris Corporation, of Melbourne, Florida.[2] In this technique, a sampling of customers is asked for two responses (each on a scale of 0 to 10) to a number of product and service queries (e.g., on-time delivery or price). The first response provides the customer's rating of the importance of that query, while the second provides the customer's rating of the company's performance for the same query. The difference between the two responses, or the gap, has been found to indicate the customer's degree of satisfaction. Gaps of less than 1 reflect a well-satisfied repeat customer, while gaps above 2 reflect a customer that is so dissatisfied, it will ac-

---

[2]"Do You Really Know What Your Customer Wants?" *Electronic Business*, p. 73–78, Oct. 1992.

tively seek ways to replace the company's products wherever practical.

A second method, reported by AVX Corporation of Myrtle Beach, South Carolina, uses a customer satisfaction index (CSI) to rate its products in seven categories (reliability, delivery, availability, price, responsiveness, support, performance, product literature, and ease of doing business).[3] The customer is first asked to distribute 100 points among these categories based on the importance of the category; this is a weighting factor. The customer is then asked to indicate AVX's performance for each category on a rating of 0 to 10. The product of the two responses produces an overall effectiveness score (the CSI), which is expressed as a percentage. For both methods, a follow-up call by a product-line representative is usually made to any customer that expresses serious problems or concerns.

Whichever method a company prefers, nearly 70 percent of the companies that participated in the 1992 *Electronic Business* quality survey indicated that they monitor customer satisfaction in one way or another.[4] Five years earlier, only a handful of the enlightened would have responded affirmatively.

Since we have shown repeatedly that effective product development begins and ends with the customer, such surveys represent a useful way to invite their comments and concerns. Customer responses take on special importance during the early phases of product introduction, when rapid feedback is needed for surfacing potential problems.

Process characterization

This is a particularly powerful tool to simplify complex processes that often add unnecessary cycle time delays. Here, a facilitator interviews the members of an organization

---

[3]ibid., p. 76.

[4]"What is Return on Quality, and Why you Should Care," *Electronic Business*, p. 60–66, Oct. 1992.

to learn how its day-to-day activities are carried out from the perspective of process efficiency, the results of which are portrayed in a process flow diagram.[5] The as-is diagram (shown in Figure 6.2a) highlights current bottlenecks, redundancies, or other problem areas. The members of the organization then work with the facilitator to draft an improved (should-be) process flow (shown in Figure 6.2b) as well as a plan to bring the organization toward it. In the hands of a skilled facilitator, this approach is powerful—accomplishing overall efficiencies while building a stronger, motivated work team. Process characterization is especially effective for enabling technology and product development groups to streamline the administrative aspects of their work.

Benchmarking

The central concept of benchmarking is to compare your performance and processes with those of companies with proven excellence in the same area of interest. Most U.S. companies have participated to some extent in benchmarking activities, often as part of a companywide TQM thrust for continuous improvement. Therefore, many such efforts are in areas that are not directly related to development—including purchasing practices, distribution methods, advertising, strategic planning, and manufacturing approaches. Moreover, companies chosen for benchmarking need not be in the same field, for the process is the focus of such efforts. Consequently, many companies have benchmarked L. L. Bean for product distribution, 3-M for innovation, Motorola for quality, and Mary Kay Cosmetics for inventory control. The few companies (seventeen between 1988 and 1992) that have won the coveted Malcolm Baldrige quality award are in great demand for benchmarking collaboration; it is said

---

[5]M. E. Martinez, "Process Characterization: the First Step in Improving Customer Satisfaction," *Transactions of the 14th Annual AQP Spring Conference and Resource Mart,* op. cit., p. 511–515.

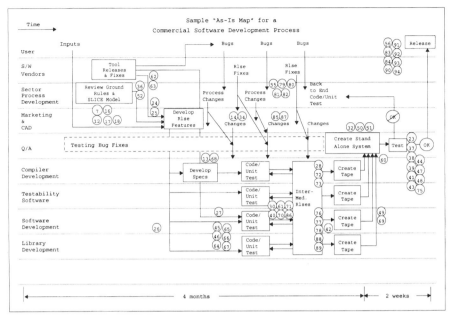

a. As-is chart

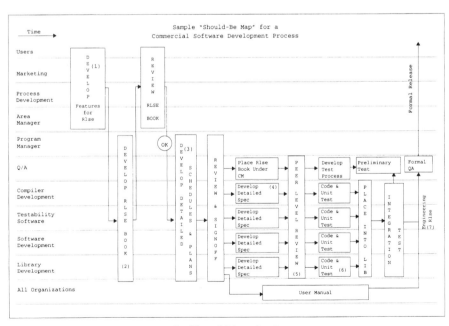

b. Should-be chart

FIGURE 6.2. Process characterization flow charts.

SOURCE: Courtesy of Harris Corporation, Melbourne, FL.

TABLE 6.2. Three major types of benchmarking activities.

Type	Description
Internal	Focus is on your own company's processes. Metrics can be compared with values in the public literature, from employees, or from consultants.
External competitive	Comparison of your own company's metrics and processes with competitors in the same industry.
External noncompetitive	Comparison of your company's metrics and processes with companies having demonstrated world-class performance in specific areas—regardless of the company's field of business.

that these 17 award winners have collectively made 10,000 public presentations on this subject to other industry groups.[6]

Recently, some companies are beginning to benchmark the product development process, and such practices are of utmost interest to the theme of this book. As indicated in Table 6.2, there are three types of benchmarking that are appropriate for the development process: internal, external competitive, and external noncompetitive, with most companies using these in sequence as they gain benchmarking experience. Initial benchmarking efforts should be directed inward, in order to fully understand your own company's capabilities before comparing them with another. The metrics used to benchmark product and technology development are discussed in chapter 7 and include parameters such as break-even time, new product sales, development cycle time, and product designs per engineer.

A suggested sequence of events to carry out a benchmarking activity on product or technology development is listed below:

---

[6]"ISO 9000 Saps Energy from Baldrige," *Electronic Business Buyer*, p. 106, Oct. 1993.

- Select a small benchmarking team and a champion to lead the effort. Team members should be experienced, process-oriented, and have good interactive skills.

- Based on discussions with product and technology development personnel (and their customers) as well as on an assessment of existing development data, select a specific area to benchmark. Candidates might be CAD tools, test procedures, assembly procedures, or product definition. Although benchmarking the effectiveness (and efficiency) of the total development process will surely be suggested, it is advisable to start on a smaller specific subtask. The experience gained will be invaluable for launching a subsequent effort to benchmark the entire process. Of course, try to select an area in which improvement will lead to a major enhancement of your overall development effectiveness.

- Document the specific process currently used in your own company. Identify areas that your own employees are concerned about.

- Establish a quantitative baseline of performance for the target area, with two or three agreed-upon, easy-to-understand metrics (see chapter 7). Attempt to determine the major reasons for any metrics that are especially poor.

- Through discussions with employees, colleagues, consultants, or professional contacts, identify companies to approach for possible benchmarking.

- Contact these companies and determine their interest in benchmarking with you or with a group of companies that include yours. Be sure to communicate your organization's willingness to participate in open and candid discussions, based on quantitative metrics and a thorough understanding of your process.

- After the initial benchmarking meeting, follow-up responsibly to build mutual trust. This will increase the chances for continuation of the effort or for extending it to other areas.

- Implement appropriate process changes and metrics to monitor progress. Benchmarking is just another technique for the identification of opportunities. Its real value lies in the implementation of subsequent process change. Benchmarking and then not making any changes is worse than not benchmarking at all.

Activity-based cost accounting

One might wonder why any accounting approach would be covered in a discussion on product and technology development. The answer is simply that all business practices are driven by the impact on the organization's bottom line, and activity-based accounting provides useful and accurate guidance regarding development expenses.

A recent survey by the National Center for Manufacturing Sciences (NCMS) showed that nearly half of the employees of U.S. manufacturing companies do not understand their current accounting systems.[7] Such systems are usually based on direct labor costs, despite the fact that labor is a rapidly shrinking fraction of many of our technology-oriented businesses. Twenty-five years ago, labor accounted for as much as 40 percent of productions costs—today, it is closer to 5 percent.[8] The same NCMS survey indicated that 52 percent of the U.S. companies surveyed are considering a change in their accounting system—presumably to one based on functional activities.

Activity-based cost accounting breaks down expenses into functional product, technology, or process categories.

---

[7]"New NCMS Initiative Puts Power of Collaboration to Work in Corporate Accounting Departments," *Focus* (National Center for Manufacturing Sciences, Ann Arbor, MI), p. 4–5, Oct. 1993.

[8]Ibid., p. 8.

For example, traditional accounting methods might allocate the expenses of a development program into broad financial categories, such as those listed in the left column of Table 6.3. ABC instead uses categories like the ones listed in the right column. Armed with information relating specific operations to specific costs, the development team can assess the relative value and cost associated with each technical operation. Since performance metrics are usually related to the efficient use of a company's resources (both people and dollars), activity-based costs can provide direct and near-real-time feedback about such resources. Not surprisingly, operational bottlenecks that drive up costs often are found to be the same ones that drive up development completion time!

In the United States, approximately 25 percent of manufacturing companies are said to use some form of ABC, with that fraction growing rapidly as its value continues to be recognized. Interestingly, Japan does not currently use ABC techniques.

Unfortunately, the conversion of a traditional cost accounting system to activity-based accounting is a considerable chore, one that might involve the entire financial organization and require a substantial investment of time and money. Once established, however, it helps middle managers and supervisors assume direct responsibility for their daily operations (and costs).

TABLE 6.3. **Example of traditional versus activity-based cost accounting.**

Traditional cost accounting	Activity-based cost accounting
• Salaries	• Process development
• Travel	• Design and layout
• Supplies	• Inspection
• Maintenance	• Testing
• Subcontractor services	• Qualification
• Overhead	• Assembly
	• Training and education

Reengineering

This is a recent variant of process characterization, with an emphasis on the radical redesign of business processes. According to Hammer and Champy, in simple terms, it means starting over.[9] It begins with a clean sheet of paper, ignoring current practices. However, reengineering is still primarily concerned with processes; hence, it is imperative that the strategic issues and directions be resolved first. Know the what and why of doing something before determining how to do it. Several practical suggestions for reengineering are listed below:[10]

- Get the strategy straight first. Don't waste time on things that shouldn't be done in the first place.

- Executive buy-in is essential. Since radical process departures will probably span several functional operations, top-level leadership is critical.

- Invoke a sense of urgency. This can be triggered from several sources, but the most effective is from a major customer.

- Work from the outside in. Start from the perspective of your customer, whether internal or external.

- Combine top-down and bottom-up initiatives. Any change will need employee involvement. Use the folks who know the best—but charge them from the top.

Sweeping process changes can be costly, and reengineering should be considered carefully before proceeding; however, the business payoff from an innovative, revolutionary process redirection can be huge. In most cases,

---

[9]Michael Hammer and James Champy, *Reengineering the Corporation,* (New York, Harper, 1993) p. 31.

[10]T.A. Stewart, "Reengineering—the Hot New Management Tool," *Fortune,* p. 41–47, Aug. 23, 1993.

reengineering results in dramatic productivity improvements—that is, ways are often found for accomplishing a specific task with less resources, or eliminating some tasks entirely. In either case, the outcome is usually a reduction in costs and personnel.

Concurrent engineering

This approach is a natural by-product of self-directed work teams. At the heart of each is a development team having a broad range of necessary functional skills (e.g., design, manufacturing, quality, and marketing), and empowered to carry out a program from definition to completion. The principal strength of this approach is that it puts the power to make things happen into the hands of the people who know the most about it. Moreover, by making the team multifunctional, it is more apt to anticipate potential problems throughout all stages of development, as described in chapters 3 and 4.

> Concurrent engineering is based on cooperation, synergy, frequent communication, and the anticipation of potential business and technology problems.

The magnitude of improvement that has been obtained from concurrent development (and self-directed work teams) is illustrated in Table 6.4, which is taken from an eleven-company study carried out by the Institute for Defense Analysis.[11] From these results, as well as many others, it is not uncommon to see up to three-fold reductions in development times after self-directed work teams and a concurrent development methodology are established.

For *product development*, multifunctional teams are frequently embraced. However, for *enabling technology development*, they are used less often. According to the Arthur D.

---

[11]Institute for Defense Analysis, IDA Report R-338, Alexandria, VA, Dec. 1988.

TABLE 6.4. Benefits obtained from the use
of concurrent development.

Benefit	Amount
• Reduced development cycle time	40–60%
• Reduced manufacturing cost	30–40%
• Reduced scrap and rework	75%
• Reduced engineering change orders during production	50%

SOURCE: R.I. Winner et al, *The Role of Concurrent Engineering in Weapons System Acquisition* (Institute for Defense Analysis, Alexandria, VA, December 1988).

Little study described in chapter 2, the use of self-directed work teams is the single-most-cited activity to enhance product innovation.

TOOLS FOR PRODUCT AND TECHNOLOGY DEVELOPMENT

Quality function deployment (QFD)

Meeting customer needs is the name of the game. As we have shown throughout this book, one of the major characteristics of the new product and technology development paradigm is that development is pulled by the market and customer—not pushed by technologists. There are two important steps in meeting customer needs: the first is determining the nature of the needs, and the second is translating them to product specifications and overall capabilities. Neither is easy.

In fact, determining the customer's requirements can be quite difficult; many of them may not even be stated in direct, candid discussions with the customer. In his book on concurrent engineering, Shina describes the following distinctly different types of customer specifications:[12]

---

[12]S. Shina, *Concurrent Engineering and Design for Manufacturing of Electronic Products* (Van Nostrand Reinhold, New York, 1991) p. 149–50.

- *Essential* requirements are often unspoken, but are so basic to the customer that no product will be considered that doesn't satisfy 100 percent of these characteristics (e.g., a full gas tank for a car rental business). Such requirements will dissatisfy the customer if unfulfilled; but they will not provide differentiating value if fulfilled.

- *Standard specifications* are the specific items that the customer has carefully considered. They provide satisfaction if met and dissatisfaction if not. These will usually be discussed by the customer in some detail.

- *Breakthrough specifications* are qualities the customer may not have even thought of. The customer may feel that they are unrealistic and may not even be able to express them very well. Providing such benefits can only create greater customer satisfaction.

However difficult it may be to determine the customer's needs, the extent to which an organization accomplishes it will probably have a direct bearing on the overall chance of the product's success.

Having once determined the customer requirements, an experienced product engineer may be able to perform many of the translations to product requirements quite directly. But as product complexity increases, so do the multiple trade-offs between its possible features and customer specifications. Consequently, a systematic approach to explore such trade-offs is valuable. Quality function deployment (QFD) is a planning and analysis tool for just that purpose. It provides a formal method for identifying user requirements and translating these into an optimal subset from among a multitude of possible design choices.

Quality function deployment was developed by the Japanese in the '60s, and applied to their product development in the early '70s. It was promoted in Japan by Yoji Akao of Tamagawa University, and was eventually picked up by U.S. companies in the mid '80s—notably in the automotive industry.[13] Since then, it has been applied to both hardware and software products in leading-edge companies and has come to be recognized as an important contributor to sound product definition.

The main contribution of QFD is optimally matching development activities and product features to customer requirements. It ensures that a development team's limited resources will be applied to those areas in which they will really count—in the eyes of the customer!

The following analysis is carried out beginning with the assumption of a reasonable understanding of the customer's requirements, including essential, standard, and breakthrough specifications. In Figure 6.3, we illustrate a QFD analysis for a fictitious company developing a personal computer targeted for desktop publishing applications. Customer requirements are first determined (first column), and each is weighed in importance relative to the

		Product capabilities								
Customer requirements	Customer Weighting	Video accelerator card	Hard drive speed	Monitor size and resolution	Microprocessor speed	Local BUS	RAM memory size	Power supply capacity	CDROM drive	Hard-drive capacity
Good image quality	40%	⊕		⊕						
Fast scrolling	30%	⊕	⊕		⊕	+	+	+		
Multimedia capability	20%	+	+		+	+	+	+	⊕	
Price sensitivity	10%				-	-	⊕	-		-
Total score	100%	5.5	2.7	2.5	2.4	2.2	1.2	1.5	1.4	-.3

Relationships
⊕ Very strong positive = 7
+ Strong positive = 3
- Strong negative = -3

FIGURE 6.3. Quality function deployment (QFD) relationships for a fictitious PC maker.

[13]Y. Akao, *Quality Function Deployment: Integrating Customer Requirements into Product Design* (Productivity Press, Cambridge, MA, 1990).

others (second column). Then each possible product characteristic is examined against customer requirements, and the strength of each relationship is denoted symbolically. A scoring algorithm is devised to quantify the analysis (bottom row). The results of such an exercise highlight the areas of greatest importance in the development program; in this case, accelerator cards, hard disk drive speed, and monitor size and resolution were found to be the most important product areas for attention.

After determining this first-order set of product characteristics, the analysis can be extended to ever-increasing detail in the product characteristics—for example, the specific types of hard disk drives (e.g., memory capacity, access time, and disk diameter) can be evaluated. QFD can also be effectively used to extend the customer requirements to technology, processing and manufacturing options. Specifically, a QFD analysis might be useful for evaluating product characteristics versus technology characteristics—then technology characteristics versus process—then process versus manufacturing, and so on. In this way, the customer's requirements are translated throughout every nook and cranny of the development organization. QFD is said to be an extension of the voice of the customer. Such a progression is indicated in Figure 6.4.

The importance of QFD is not the analysis itself, for such quantification is still somewhat subjective. It is, however, a tool that can be used by a work team to carefully consider all of the development options against definitive customer input and help the team translate the voice of the customer into specific product development activities.

Comparing design options

Closely related to QFD is a technique in which product options are compared side by side against the current product approach. Although there are many possible variations, one simple method is illustrated in Table 6.5a. Here, the customer requirements are listed in the first column, with

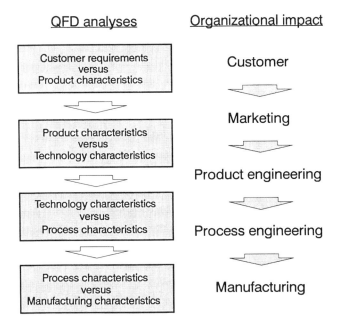

FIGURE 6.4. Extension of QFD analyses to additional elements of the overall product development process.

the current product entered as the baseline in the second column. In subsequent columns, several other product options are compared with the current approach—with a rating of better (+), the same (N), or worse (–) indicated for each customer requirement and for each product design option. In the bottom row, the number of pluses and minuses are added to indicate the best choices (options 1 and 4 for this example).

A slightly more complex variation of the same analysis is illustrated in Table 6.5b. In this case, the various customer requirements are weighed in importance (column 2), and each design option is compared with the current approach through a quantitative score of 1 to 10 (with 5 being neutral). The final scores in the bottom row are simply a weighed summation.

Whatever methodology is preferred, an analysis such as this complements QFD by helping a work team to compare the pros and cons of several product options under consideration.

TABLE 6.5. Comparing product design options relative to a current approach.

	Current design	Design option				
		1	2	3	4	5
Speed	N	+	+	N	N	–
Reliability	N	N	N	+	+	–
Power consumption	N	+	–	N	N	–
Manufacturing cost	N	+	–	N	+	N
Weight	N	N	–	–	N	+
Horsepower	N	+	N	+	+	N
Relative scores		4 +	1 +	2 +	3 +	1 +
		0 –	3 –	1 –	1 –	3 –

a. simple

	Weighing factor	Current design	Design option				
			1	2	3	4	5
Speed	.25	5	8	7	5	5	3
Reliability	.15	5	5	5	9	8	2
Power consumption	.15	5	7	3	5	5	4
Manufacturing cost	.30	5	9	2	5	8	5
Weight	.10	5	5	1	3	5	6
Horsepower	.05	5	7	5	8	9	5
Relative Scores	1.00	5.00	7.35	3.90	5.55	6.55	4.0

b. complex

Design reuse

As product designers grow in expertise and professional maturity, they naturally build upon previous experience—primarily their own, and perhaps to some extent that of their close associates. Bits and pieces of earlier assignments are informally and opportunistically reused, providing modest productivity enhancements along the way.

Over the past decade, the widespread use of computer-based design tools has impacted virtually all development methodologies, and the reusable character of software has made design reuse important. At the component level, computer-aided design (CAD) libraries have been established that house collections of cells and arrays—the building blocks of semiconductor products. Taking the library concept one step higher, component modules are similarly integrated in the design of printed-circuit boards and electronic sub-systems. And programming code is now often broken into segments for selective integration in mammoth software design projects, at considerable resource savings.

However, design reuse is not as straightforward as it may appear, for the reusable information must be easily understood, despite the fact that it was created by the earlier work of another. Standard interfaces and configurations as well as documentation procedures and formats must be agreed upon. A potential user can otherwise spend considerable effort attempting to understand the features, limitations, and interfaces of a reusable model. Moreover, such a reusable module might be prepared quite differently than one intended for a single application—without regard for reuse.

For design reuse to be worthwhile, an organization must establish a set of standards that apply to all information (i.e., code, cells, modules) that is to be retained for community reuse. Such standards provide guidelines for the following information:

- Characteristics.

- Intended applications.

- Limitations.

- Documentation and reference literature.

- Format.

- Originator.

- Additional support (i.e., a person to contact for help).

Obviously, a considerable amount of extra work is needed to meet the standards listed above, and a case-by-case decision must be made regarding placement of information into a design library. Consideration should be based on the amount of effort required to support reuse, the likelihood of its future use, and the expected organizational savings. In many advanced development organizations, an ad-hoc team of experienced designers is chartered to oversee a reuse library on behalf of the organization.

The bottom line is that design reuse must be taken seriously, for it will be used with increasing frequency as more and more products are designed with computer tools or elaborate software code. In such cases, the benefits in employee productivity and design cycle time will justify the efforts required to establish a reuse activity. Moreover, as product designs continue to become more complex, the only way to rationally integrate the growing number of components is to break the design into (reusable) subsections, thereby adding further impetus to the need for this capability.

Technology transfer

The use of empowered work teams dramatically changes the nature of product and technology transfers. In traditional development programs, several transfers occur in nearly every development program. For example:

- Technology transfer from the R&D center to the advanced development lab or to the factory.

- Product transfer from design to manufacturing, and again from manufacturing to marketing and sales. Each is typically a hand-off of responsibility, as described earlier in chapter 4.

After the product is in volume production, other transfers between manufacturing facilities or between different manufacturing lines in a single facility are not uncommon. For any and all transfers of this type there are two cardinal rules, which experience has shown should not be transgressed—though the temptation to do so is often enormous.

- *Rule 1:* Transfer key people along with a process. Such a transfer need not be permanent, but it should be sufficiently long to ensure that the transition is successful.

- *Rule 2:* Transfer a process (and type of equipment) as an exact copy of the original. Avoid the temptation to improve the process until it has convincingly demonstrated its previous behavior. Senior factory and engineering personnel wear many scars from this mistake.

Although the use of multifunctional work teams has considerably reduced handing off responsibilities during the development process, the rules above are still valid for any transfers that are required.

Innovation

Most of this book describes the new development paradigm from the perspective of achieving steady progress toward agreed-upon objectives. Use of a formal (i.e., written) development process with clear objectives and appropriate metrics helps ensure that all the logical steps of the process are carried out effectively. But such a process may not do justice to one important element of research and development—innovation. Spontaneous, creative ideas often provide startling, revolutionary approaches that leapfrog current products or technologies. They account for 3M's Post-Its® and Sony's Walk-Man®. Who first conceived chewing gum? Or paper clips? Or white-out?

Although the marvels of the human creative thought process lie beyond the author's expertise, the approaches described below have been found to be helpful to apply such thinking to development activities.

Creative reflection

New approaches or fresh insights often occur spontaneously, and usually not during normal work hours. Such ideas do, however, seem to just happen, but often during rather similar activities:

- Driving to work.
- Showering or bathing.
- Just before falling asleep.
- Taking a walk or jogging.
- Listening to instrumental music.

In each of these cases, the mind is relaxed—only mildly occupied with the routine task of the moment and free from the many incoming signals that characterize our normal business schedule. Hence, the issue comes down to stimulating the creative thought process in a work environment. The following business practices may enhance such thinking:

- Hold planning sessions off site, in a quiet, relaxed environment. Discourage interruptions, and allow ample time for thinking. Keep work groups small and noncompetitive.

- For personal reflection, allow time each day to reexamine overall directions and approaches. Such thinking should be similarly uninterrupted. Some managers arrive early for work and restrict interruptions for perhaps the first 30 minutes of the day.

- When reflecting, concentrate on the big picture. Extend the thought process as far as possible. By all means, don't waste reflection on details. Also, keep the thoughts positive—avoiding initial consideration of barriers.

- Take down notes about fresh ideas immediately afterward. Don't wait for a convenient time, for some of the elements won't be recalled later (the mind's funny that way).

We can indicate one final factor that prohibits novel thinking. A fresh approach to a problem will usually not surface when you are in the midst of the problem itself. At such times your mind is too locked into a particular direction to see any other way. If something is put down (and forgotten) for a day or so, and then reexamined, new approaches often appear.

Brainstorming and problem solving

Experienced development personnel often find they can best resolve project difficulties or identify new approaches through brainstorming. Such an activity is especially effective in small work teams, ideally with two to three people who are open with one another. In such a session, the objective is to identify alternatives for a current or future issue. The following guidelines may be helpful:

- Use a white board or chalkboard, so that ideas can easily be moved around into categories or expanded.

- Don't restrict contributions. Jot down all suggestions somewhere—even if they are initially thought to be a little off the subject.

- Write legibly. Ideas that can't be read can't be reinforced or expanded.

- When everything useful seems to have been captured, make a second pass over the material, enhancing it in the following ways:

— Add the overall objective.
— Sort the responses into categories.
— Add specifics (topic by topic) one level deeper into the subject.
— Add action items that come to mind.
— Summarize results.
— Copy and distribute to participants.

Computer software is now available to promote brainstorming—even for an individual. Although such tools can be helpful in extending a person's thoughts into new areas, it is a weak substitute for the person-to-person synergy that can be captured by a small team of knowledgeable and motivated individuals.

Tapping the customer

In several conversations with product and market development individuals, a single conclusion became clear.[14] Most useful ideas for new products come from the customer. This is not really surprising, since the customer in most cases is the end user—or represents the end user. Close customer interactions therefore not only enhance the product or technology undergoing development, but also provide direction for future products!

Knowing this, a company can foster product innovation by promoting and organizing activities that involve the customer. Examples of such activities are:

• Focus group meetings.

• Telephone surveys.

• Customer training sessions.

---

[14]This idea was especially evident during a conversation with Gary Tighe of Harris Semiconductor, who benchmarked product innovation with several other U.S. companies in the semiconductor and electronics industries.

- Industry conferences and workshops that are attended by customers.

- Company seminars.

- Sales and marketing trip reports.

- Application engineering reports.

- Response to advertisements.

- Program or project reviews with the customer.

- Supplier rating meetings.

These activities are not novel. But the important idea here is that such activities are sprinkled with the best product ideas that are likely to surface. All efforts should be made to harvest these ideas thoroughly. All too often, trip reports, advertisement responses, and the like get filed without any organized review. A concerted effort must be taken to collect such ideas, since the input is usually obtained at different times by different people and from a variety of different sources.

> Listen to the customer; he or she can provide not only guidance about your current project, but also the very best ideas for future products!

IN SUMMARY

The paradigm shift in product and technology development is often captured under such corporate umbrellas as TQM (total quality management) and concurrent engineering. TQM focuses on doing the job right—any job—and attacks this broad objective with activities in customer satisfaction, continuous improvement, and process characterization. Each of these is directly applicable to product or technology development. Customer satisfaction surveys clearly indicate when an organization is not cutting it. Activity-based cost accounting systems also can help pinpoint financial bottlenecks and waste. Enabling technology development organizations can especially benefit from the use of process characterization—an activity that establishes process flow charts and action programs to advance from the way things are to the way they should be. And benchmarking with external organizations during the development process is strongly recommended as an initial step for implementing process change.

A few tools included in this chapter are unique in their applications to product or technology development. Quality function deployment (QFD) is an analytical technique that systematically identifies and prioritizes product areas that most closely support the customer's needs. Design reuse is growing in importance as technically oriented businesses are finding it important to capture some of their design efforts in modules for subsequent use. Finally, some guidance is provided to enhance innovative thinking as well as technology transfer.

CHAPTER 7

Measuring

Progress

THE IMPORTANCE
OF GOOD METRICS

The journey to world-class product and technology development is arduous at best. It's especially difficult if you don't know your origin, or the speed and direction of your travel. The selection of appropriate metrics determines both the starting point (baseline) and the necessary landmarks (progress) to move along the trail as quickly as possible.

An old adage relating to product or technology development is simply stated:

> Inspect what you expect.

In other words, establishing a metric and consistently and visibly reviewing it indicate sufficient management importance to help bring about its improvement. Bill Hewlett, co-founder of Hewlett-Packard, is quoted as saying, "You can't manage what you can't measure," and

"What gets measured, gets done."[1] However it's said, the message is clear.

A small set of properly established metrics can provide the following benefits for product and technology development:

- They establish a real-time measure of progress toward meeting the final objectives.

- They communicate a message that the subject is important to management and the development team.

- They provide a rallying point, especially if the metrics are highly visible to the team and its peers.

The attributes of a good metric (or set of metrics) are summarized in Table 7.1. Although these characteristics seem straightforward, metrics are often poorly used. First, any metric that is devised or selected should monitor only the essential factors, avoiding detailed second-order distractions (nuisance factors). It is important that maximum insights be gleaned with a minimum amount of data, and that the data be relatively straightforward to access. If the data is difficult to collect or it is perceived to provide little value, the process will understandably cause more resent-

TABLE 7.1.

Attributes of an effective metric.

- The metric captures the most essential factors.
- It monitors those factors with minimum data and organizational disruption.
- The metric can be presented graphically in a way that easily conveys relative progress.
- It is (or can be) standardized over all similar organizations.
- The metric is examined regularly, and used to guide improvements.

---

[1] C. H. House and R. L. Price, "The Return Map: Tracking Product Teams," *Harvard Business Review,* p. 92–100, Jan.–Feb. 1991.

ment than assistance. Similarly, the metric should be useful to the group being monitored (in contrast to a corporate or external organization).

Before any metric is implemented, it should be considered carefully from several different perspectives, because it will almost certainly result in behavioral changes—whether or not they are the ones desired. An old story is told about a productivity study of a group of typists. Counters were attached to their terminals to determine how many keystrokes were being entered each day. After a few days, the measured number of keystrokes was found to increase dramatically—until someone discovered that the major behavioral change was the typists' lunch routine; they now ate at their desks while holding down the space bar!

Finally, the most important attribute of any metric is that it be used! Technologists frequently cite one or another management fire drills to gather a certain set of data, which subsequently disappears into the corporate black hole. No one learns of the outcome, nor is there any follow-up in the form of action programs. Unless an organization is committed to improvement and willing to publicly share the results of the data, it is better not to initiate such an activity.

PRODUCT DEVELOPMENT
CYCLE TIME

The most basic development metric is simply the time it takes to complete the development cycle. But this parameter must be defined carefully, because there are several different possibilities for specifying the starting and completion points, including:

- Beginning the measurement immediately after a product candidate has passed the initial product concept screening.

- Beginning the measurement after approval of the product candidate's business plan.

- Ending the completion time immediately after the product is transferred to manufacturing.

- Ending the completion time when the product is available for customer purchase.

These are illustrated conceptually in Figure 7.1.

The proper choice of the starting and ending points for a development cycle time metric should be made carefully, based on two organizational considerations: the metric's potential for producing organizational change, and its difficulty in implementing.

From Figure 7.1, the increment labeled concept-to-market time is conceptually the best, because it captures the largest portion of the total product development cycle. It especially captures the two parts of the process that have traditionally been the weakest for U.S. companies—product definition and market introduction. However, this definition is also the most difficult to implement because of the need for starting the clock before the technical part of the development is officially approved (after

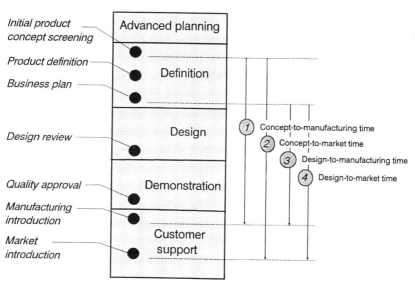

FIGURE 7.1. Options for defining the product development cycle time.

the business plan review) and for stopping the clock at market introduction, a time outside the horizon of traditional development engineers. In contrast, the design-to-manufacturing time is the simplest to implement and is probably the closest to any historical cycle time data that may exist.

In my opinion, the most important point is to immediately begin monitoring some form of development cycle time, if it is not already being done. The second most important point is to use the metric that captures the largest part of the cycle that is reasonably accessible, rather than waiting to develop a capability to have a better metric. Progress is relative, not absolute.

However, the eventual goal should clearly be to capture the entire cycle from the beginning of the product definition activity to the point at which the product is available for customers to purchase. Any missing portions of the cycle should be added to the metric at the earliest opportunity, for the more difficult elements to implement are probably those with the greatest opportunity for improvement.

OWNERSHIP

A final note should be added before addressing a variety of specific metrics. The ownership of metrics should be at the highest level possible—at least at a division level for multidivisional corporations. Even though various product lines can champion a specific set of metrics, it is better if the successful ones are incorporated as widely as possible throughout the division or corporation. Moreover, product-oriented groups are continually subjected to company reorganizations—the product categories of today surely won't be applicable to tomorrow. For these and other reasons, the best of all worlds is for the metrics to be embraced and widely used throughout the lowest possible company levels, but administered at the highest possible.

METRICS FOR PRODUCT AND
TECHNOLOGY DEVELOPMENT

In the area of product and technology development, metrics serve three distinctly different purposes, and should be designed differently, depending on the intended usage. One application is to provide a strategic summary of an organization's development program. Here, statistics regarding progress from year to year, the percent of long-term versus short-term investments, and overall payback are most important. The second purpose is to guide the development of active programs, signaling problems that require immediate attention. Finally, the third purpose is to gather data that allows benchmarking one organization (or company) with another. Here, industry-standard parameters must be used for meaningful comparisons. Sample metrics for each of these three purposes are described in the following sections.

Strategic assessment of
completed programs

A set of metrics that has been found to be especially useful for top-level evaluation of a group of completed product and technology programs is illustrated in Figure 7.2. This set of metrics is appropriate for assessing the balance of a company's overall development program and for determining the extent of progress over an extended period of time, for example, last year versus this year.

Development portfolio balance

Figure 7.2a establishes the development portfolio versus the type of products or technologies being developed. First-of-a-kind or company firsts are potentially high-impact products offering large financial returns. However, such products also have above-average risk (and costs) because of their technical complexity. The other categories of products are evolutionary, and generally constitute the bulk of a

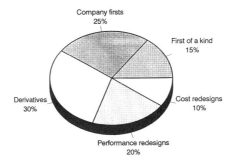

FIGURE 7.2a. Sample metric: Fictitious distribution of development products by type.

product portfolio. Their risk, investment, and potential impact are usually acceptable, but not spectacular. A simple chart like Figure 7.2a helps keep an appropriate balance between the derivatives and redesigns versus the high-investment, first-of-a-kind products.

Completion time

In Figure 7.2b, we illustrate a method of portraying the average product completion time for the same categories of product types. In reality, the times will probably vary by about a factor of two between the most complex and least complex products. The difference between the actual completion times and those forecast in an annual operating plan also can be monitored to track the overall amount of

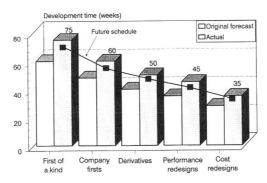

FIGURE 7.2b. Sample metric: Fictitious average development cycle time versus type of product.

slippage over the course of the program. Initially, such slippage often adds as much as 40 percent to 50 percent to the original completion estimate. However, as the new product development paradigm gains acceptance, both the absolute cycle times and the spread between original forecast and actual completion times will shrink.

The availability of data such as that in Figure 7.2b is an asset for forecasting future product development programs. For example, if this data represented the current organization's capability, and a first-of-a-kind product candidate was being defined, the team would realize that development cycle times were currently running 75 weeks (versus a forecast time of only 60 weeks). They might then choose to schedule their new development project at perhaps 71 weeks, providing an aggressive target for themselves to do better than average, but not so unrealistically short as to be beyond the organization's capabilities.

New product revenue

Figure 7.2c is perhaps the most important chart to illustrate the effectiveness of a development program. Here, the annual sales for an organization are subtotaled by the year of product introduction and charted as a stacked bar chart. In

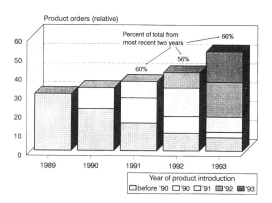

FIGURE 7.2c. Sample metric: Vintage chart showing revenue generated from new products.
SOURCE: Hewlett Packard 1993 Annual Report. Courtesy of Hewlett Packard Corporation.

this fashion, the percentage of sales based on the past two or three years can be determined and observed as a trend over a period of several years. A percentage of 30 percent to 40 percent for three years is a reasonable target for a company with a balanced portfolio of established and emerging products. Relatively mature product portfolios might produce new product contributions closer to 20 percent to 25 percent. However, percentages this low signal danger for future profitability. In contrast, products involved in fast-paced industries, such as computers, have very short life cycles, and the percent of new product revenue must provide a much higher fraction of new product sales. The example used in Figure 7.2c is taken from the 1993 Annual Report of Hewlett Packard, the electronics giant with nearly 75 percent of its revenue derived from computers.

Break-even time

In Figure 7.2d, we include a break-even analysis that was developed at Hewlett Packard and has been reported by House and Price.[2] This analysis requires data from all aspects of development: sales revenue, development costs, and profit margins. Such data is available only in companies with relatively thorough (and accessible) accounting

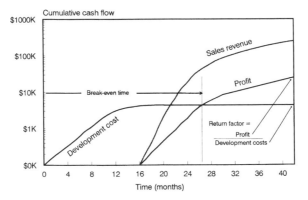

FIGURE 7.2d. Sample metric: Fictitious cost, revenue, and profit curves, illustrating break-even time and return factor.

---

[2]House and Price.

systems. However, if available, it is a valuable overall metric, because it can rate the effectiveness of a development program in terms of its actual payback. A useful process descriptor in Figure 8.2d is the break-even time—that is, the time at which sales profits match investment costs.

Return factor

This metric is defined over the entire life cycle of the product and is the ratio of the total operating profit divided by the total development cost:[3]

$$\text{Return factor} = \frac{\text{Life cycle product operating profit}}{\text{Total product development cost.}}$$

As for any other investment, the return factor provides a quantitative indication of the return on investment. To be accurate, the return factor really should take into consideration the time value of money—that is, the net present value of all future costs and profits should be calculated based on the equation:

$$\text{Present Value} = \sum_{i=1}^{n} \frac{\text{Cash flow for year } i}{(1 + r)^i}$$

Like the break-even time, analysis of the return factor is only as useful as the accuracy of the profit and cost data. The profits must be derived from sales revenues over the life of the product and margins that account for manufacturing and overhead costs. Development costs should include the direct costs of the project, including labor and material, as well as an allocated portion of indirect development costs (e.g., a portion of enabling technology development costs). Because of the difficulty in forecasting profits and costs over a multiyear period, the return factor is

[3]S. G. Shina, *Concurrent Engineering and Design for Manufacturing of Electronic Products*, p. 42

used primarily for ballpark estimates. It is also illustrated in Figure 7.2d.

In Figures 7.2a and 7.2b, we divided the organization's development portfolio into product types (e.g., first of a kind, company firsts, and cost redesigns), however other characterizations can also be useful. An alternative classification is illustrated in Figure 7.3. Here, the product portfolio is divided into quadrants based on the degree of risk (and presumably reward). A new product opportunity can be targeted for market expansion, technology expansion, or both, with the degree of difficulty or risk generally increasing in this order. Hence, an alternative product characterization is:

- Defense of current business.

- Market expansions.

- Technology expansions.

- New ventures.

The final choice of a product classification must be based on the specifics of the business and on the organization's strategic focus.

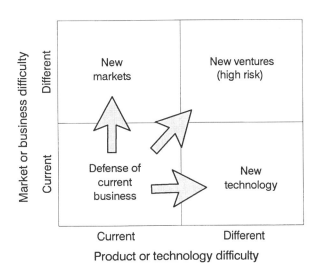

FIGURE 7.3. Product categories based on risk-reward assessment.

Programs undergoing development

In Figure 7.4, we illustrate a set of metrics that are best suited for monitoring a group of active programs. The purpose of such charts is to flag problem areas and indicate programs or functional areas in which additional focus would optimally shorten the development cycle.

Completion to schedule

In Figure 7.4a, the actual number of completions each month is compared with the number that was forecast to be completed at the beginning of the planning period. The advantage of such a metric is its focus on bringing the products to completion on or ahead of schedule. Like many metrics, its disadvantage is that it encourages lengthening the completion forecast. A graph such as Figure 7.4a must be used to discover and resolve problems—not blame people for missing forecasts. Close tracking of the overall completion times (such as those in Figure 7.2b) is required to ensure that development cycle times are dropping, rather than forecast times lengthening.

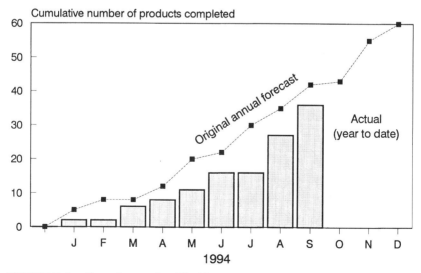

FIGURE 7.4a. Sample metric: Fictitious number of products completed year-to-date versus annual plan.

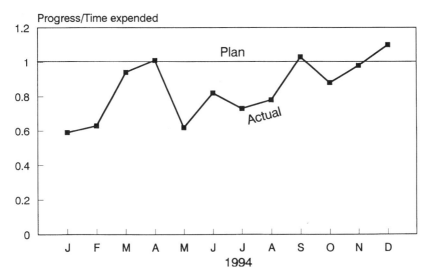

FIGURE 7.4b. Sample metric: Fictitious development productivity, as defined by the monthly progress toward completion of schedule normalized per month of expended effort.

Monthly productivity

Figure 7.4b shows a metric that can be used to monitor productivity—defined here as the amount of progress made toward completing the program divided by the actual time expended. In this chart, the forecast completion date of an active program is reexamined each period (e.g., each month). If the forecast completion date remains unchanged over that month, one month of schedule progress is assumed to have been made to go along with the one month of expended time. Such a case would therefore have a productivity ratio of unity. A one-month slip in schedule in the one-month period would score zero, while a two-month slip would score –1. The chart illustrated here might represent a collection of several individual products being carried out within a specific product development organization.

Slippage

Figure 7.4c illustrates a Pareto diagram that is convenient for determining the major functional areas responsible for

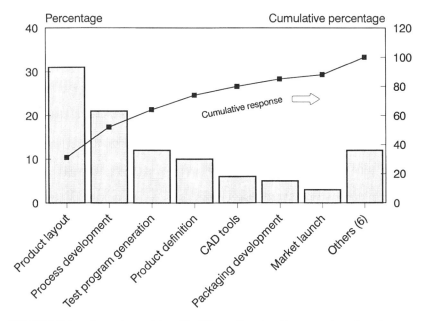

FIGURE 7.4c. Sample metric: Fictitious Pareto diagram showing the source of program slippage for a collection of products.

slippage in a collection of product development programs. If data is collected each month, and if engineers are required to specify the cause of any slips (within a set of predefined functional categories), the data will quickly reveal the process bottlenecks. Process characterization (described in chapter 7) can then be applied to the bottlenecks in an attempt to reduce the overall development cycle time.

Benchmarking R&D Performance

The third application for metrics is to compare a company's development performance and progress against competition and against best-in-class, as discussed in the previous chapter. Such comparisons are often carried out by subcontractors that specialize in collecting benchmarking data. However, a better way to compare product development practices (and performance) is to arrange a series of benchmarking sessions with one or more competitors to share insights, best practices, and current status. In today's increasingly open environment, such arrangements are feasible and mutually beneficial, as long as all participants are willing to give as much as they get, and as long as the performance levels of the companies (in the benchmarking area) are reasonably close to each other.

Whether a company is interested in a formal benchmarking study or wishes instead to compare its performance with data from the open literature, it is important to first have a good grasp of its own baseline of performance. One would think that such information would already be known—but this is usually not the case. Engineers (like golfers and fisherman) tend to remember their best (and often singular) performance, and only a set of statistically meaningful data should be used to reach a conclusion about the average status of product or technology development programs. Some of the charts illustrated in Figure 7.2 are appropriate for this, but they should be complemented with other metrics, such as those listed in Table 7.2.

Metrics that portray whether or not a company is choosing the correct products (making the right products) obviously must involve sales revenue. The ratio of new product revenue to total revenue discussed earlier (Figure 7.2c) provides a forecast of the company's future expectations. A related metric would evaluate the investment balance between high-risk, first-of-a-kind products (home runs) and conservative derivative products (singles and doubles).

The total amount of investment in R&D for a company or for an industry is available in trade journals or from the consolidated income statements that appear in most company's annual reports. R&D investment is usually specified as a percentage of sales, and ranges from less than 1 percent for mature industries like oil and steel to greater than 10 percent for high-tech growth industries like drugs, semiconductors, and computers. The R&D/sales ratios for several selected U.S. industries are listed in Table 7.3. Also included here is the R&D expense per employee, which ranges between $1,000 and $20,000 for the same industries.

TABLE 7.2. Industry-standard metrics appropriate for benchmarking a company's development status against competition.

Metric	Units	Comments
Doing the right products		
• Sales revenue per product	Dollars	By product type (first of a kind, company firsts, and derivatives) and total products.
• New product sales revenue versus total revenue	Percentage	See Figure 7.2c.
• Product investment balance	Percentage	Ratio of first of a kind plus company firsts products to total products. Numerical ratio and cost ratio.
Doing the products right		
• R&D expenses (percentage of sales)	Percentage	By emerging product lines, mature product lines, and total. Percentages are representative of specific industries.
• Development cycle time	Weeks	See Figure 7.2b.
• Development cost per product	Dollars	By product type (first of a kind, company firsts, and derivatives) and by total.
• Engineers per product (or products per engineer)	—	By product type (first of a kind, company firsts, and derivatives) and by total.
• Break-even time	Months	Figure 7.2d, rolled up to represent a group of products. Requires excellent accounting and cost allocation system.
• Return factor	—	Figure 7.2d. Difficult to accurately collect all profit and development costs. Good indicator of overall financial return on R&D investment.
• First-time success	Percentage	By product type (first of a kind, company firsts, and derivatives) and by total.

TABLE 7.3. R&D investment of U.S. companies
for selected industries.

	R&D expenses per employee	R&D expenses as a percentage of sales
Large R&D investments		
• Software	$ 21,760	13.3%
• Computer communications	$ 17,839	10.8%
• Drugs and research	$ 17,017	10.3%
• Semiconductors	$ 9,924	10.3%
• Computers	$ 13,441	8.4%
Moderate R&D investments		
• Leisure time products	$ 6,714	5.1%
• Chemicals	$ 9,177	3.9%
• Auto	$ 6,823	3.7%
• Telecommunications	$ 4,852	3.6%
Small R&D investments		
• Food	$ 1,186	0.7%
• Fuel	$ 3,585	0.7%
• Steel	$ 1,287	0.7%
• Oil	$ 3,879	0.6%

SOURCE: Extracted from "A Tighter Focus for R&D," *Business Week Quality Issue*, p. 170–216, Fall 1991.

Further information on benchmarking is provided in chapter 6.

IN SUMMARY

Monitoring the progress of product and technology development programs is absolutely imperative, and the establishment of a set of easy-to-use, easy-to-understand metrics dramatically increases the likelihood that the programs will be completed on time and on budget. Many metrics can be used for this purpose, and a set similar to those illustrated in Figures 7.2a–d and 7.4 of this chapter has been found to be valuable in monitoring the overall effectiveness of a new product development program and to assess the overall strategic balance of the organization's product directions. The choice of which metrics to use must be based on the accessibility of the data, the level of maturity of the organization's product development program, and the desired focus area. Whatever the case, it is essential that R&D be carefully monitored and strongly linked to the other facets of a company's business. A single set of standardized metrics must be established and used regularly and visibly to guide an organization's progress in doing the right things right.

Contrary to the tradition in many companies to insulate R&D from the business community, interactions that help shape and synchronize business requirements and potential product and technology benefits must be nurtured at every opportunity.

CHAPTER 8

External
Collaboration

One element of the new development paradigm that is particularly relevant to technology development is the concept
of external collaboration. Since the early '80s, research and
development alliances and consortia have become ever
more important, so that today, the sharing of resources to accomplish common goals is an accepted practice for industry
development. This is especially true in precompetitive R&D,
where the objective is to share the cost (and risk) associated
with traditional (proprietary) technology development. The
need for leveraging an organization's development program
through external collaboration is important simply because
no single company has the resources to go it alone in all aspects of its technical endeavors.

Table 8.1 summarizes the trends in national and international collaboration over the past 10 years. Before approximately 1980, each U.S. company worked independently of
(and fiercely competitively with) other companies in nearly
all aspects of its business. With the formation of research
consortia in the early '80s, formal cooperation within certain segments of the U.S. industry began. With each passing
year, the extent of collaboration has increased—in an attempt to leverage the contributions of several companies to-
wards a task too large (or costly) for any one. The concept

TABLE 8.1. Trends in national and international cooperation.

Yesterday (national competition)	Today (national cooperation—international competition)	Tomorrow (international cooperation)
R&D		
• Individual companies	• National R&D consortia (SRC, MCC, USCAR, SPC, Fraunhofer Institutes)	• International R&D consortia
Manufacturing		
• Company propri-etary methods and processes • National standards	• National manufacturing methods, processes, and equipment consortia (Sematech, NCMS) • Arm's-length (foundry) international manu-facturing	• Shared, coopera-tive international manufacturing facilities*
Products		
• Individual companies • Vertical integration	• National and international alliances. • Virtual integration**	• Intense business globalization with little regard for national boundaries

*Such a shared fab, called TECH Semiconductor, is being formed in Singapore by TI, HP, Cannon, and the Singapore Economic Board. See "Multi-Company DRAM Facility," *Semiconductor International*, p. 22, June 1991.

**"The Virtual Enterprise: Your New Model for Success," *Electronics Business*, p. 153–155, March 1992.

of vertical integration within a single corporation is evolv-ing to one of virtual integration among alliance partners from different companies.[1] To accomplish this, an organiza-tion must become an integral part of the development and manufacturing plans of its important customers.

Today's climate is one of limited national cooperation in an effort to remain successful against strong international competition. Cooperation between industry, academia, and government is being vigorously promoted through a vari-

---

[1]"The Virtual Enterprise: Your New Model for Success," *Electronics Business*, p. 153–55, March 1992.

ety of U.S. government programs. For example, government funding awards are now rarely directed to a single company, but to teams, as discussed later in this chapter.

Many cooperative relationships are beginning to be formed that are international in nature. For example, three electronics giants, IBM, Siemens, and Toshiba are teaming on a multiyear development program for future generations of memory chips.[2] Honda has worked out an arrangement with Chrysler to sell American Jeeps in Japan, where four-wheel off-road vehicles are in hot demand.[3] It is reasonable to extrapolate these and other trends to a future global business community where national and regional boundaries are blurred to the point of unimportance, but that is not yet the case.

GOVERNMENT R&D POLICIES

Over the past decade, the U.S. government has gradually awakened to the need for a national science and technology policy—if not formally described as such, at least a *de facto* policy. Toward this objective, the government appears to have begun to focus on U.S. industrial growth and economic security, rather than on defense and antitrust constraints. In the last decade, a variety of programs have been initiated to promote industrial R&D investment, and these are summarized in Table 8.2.

While tax credits and direct government contracts in the early '80s were used to promote industry investment (and especially defense-related development), the recent government financial incentives and legislation summarized in Table 8.2 have been directed to the following areas:

- A gradual post-cold-war transition of the defense industry to civilian and commercial activities.

---

[2]"IBM, Toshiba, and Siemens in 256M DRAM Alliance," *Electronic News,* p. 1–4, July 1992.

[3]"The Man Who's Selling Japan on Jeeps," *Business Week,* p. 56, July 19, 1993.

TABLE 8.2. Recent federal programs to promote industrial research and development.

Federal program	Date initiated	Purpose
R&D Tax Credits	1981–86	To encourage business investment in R&D.
Small Business Innovation Research (SBIR)	1982	To strengthen the role of small businesses in federal R&D programs.
National Cooperative Research Act (NCRA)	1984	To allow joint research by competitors without automatically triggering antitrust liability.
Technology Reinvestment Project (TRP)	1986	To help smooth the transition for defense businesses to commercial and civilian activities.
Federal Technology Transfer Act (FTTA)	1986	To allow the formation of Cooperative Research and Development Agreements (CRADAs) between industry and the National Labs.
National Competitive Technology Transfer Act (NCTTA)	1989	To allow contractor-operated labs to also enter in CRADAs with industry.

SOURCE: Data extracted from *Science and Engineering Indicators—1993*, pp. 114–120

- More intense industry collaboration with universities and government agencies in research and development programs, especially in selected technical areas.

The technology areas that have been identified by the Department of Defense and the Department of Commerce as important to the U.S. national security and future economic growth are listed in Table 8.3. These areas have gradually become part of the roadmap in outlying years for federal agencies, and therefore receive special attention in defense contracts, technology reinvestment projects, and NSF and ARPA technology awards.

TABLE 8.3. Critical and emerging technology areas for the U.S.

Technology area	Department of Defense	Department of Commerce
• Advanced composites	✔	✔
• Advanced sensors	✔	✔
• Optical information processing	✔	✔
• Artificial intelligence	✔	✔
• Computational science	✔	✔
• Software development	✔	
• Superconductivity	✔	✔
• Advanced metallic structures	✔	
• Air-breathing propulsion	✔	
• Rocket propulsion	✔	

SOURCE: *Focus* (National Center for Manufacturing Sciences, Ann Arbor, MI, Sept. 1992), p. 7.

In the sections below, we highlight several different types of government-industry-university interactions that are directed at leveraging the effectiveness of the overall U.S. research and development investment. Many of these activities can be used by a particular organization to enhance the breadth or share the costs or risks of its own projects.

U.S. R&D

In 1993, the U.S. spent approximately $161B in research and development.[4] Because of the sheer size of the U.S. economy, this is far greater than the total R&D of any other nation; in fact, it represents approximately 43 percent of the R&D for the entire industrial world.[5] However, nearly 59 percent of the federal government R&D funding is for defense. If this were excluded, the total U.S. R&D would drop substantially, and Japan's non-defense R&D investment would pull much

---

[4]Science and Engineering Indicators—1993, op. cit., p. 331.

[5]Science and Engineering Indicators—1993, op. cit., p. 97. The data here is from the Organization for Economic Co-operation and Development, and includes those countries that comprise most of the world's R&D.

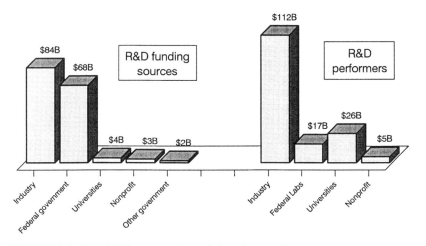

FIGURE 8.1. Total U.S. research and development.
SOURCE: Data extracted from *Science and Engineering Indicators—1993, p. 331.*

closer to that of the United States. Moreover, as a fraction of gross domestic product, the U.S. lags Japan and Germany, at 2.6 percent, 3.0 percent, and 2.8 percent, respectively.[6]

The sources of funding and the organizations that carry out the R&D in the United States are illustrated in Figure 8.1. Here, we see that most of the funds come from private industry and the federal government, with a small remainder from universities, nonprofit organizations, and state and local government. In contrast, the major R&D performers are industry and universities, with the federal government conducting about 10 percent of the U.S. R&D in its National Laboratories.

INDUSTRY-GOVERNMENT INTERACTIONS[7]

As indicated in Table 8.2, a series of legislative acts and programs have been initiated over the past decade to en-

---

[6]Ibid., p. 375.

[7]The statistics for this section were extracted from Science and Engineering Indicators—1993, op. cit., p. 114–20.

hance government support for research and development. Summarized below are the highlights of these programs and the magnitude of their impact on industrial development.

Direct government R&D contracts

This support has been a substantial contribution to the total U.S. R&D since World War II. However, after years of continued growth, direct federal contracts to private industry have been constant or slightly declining at $25B to $30B since 1987 (see Figure 8.2). In constant dollars, the decline is even more apparent. Direct federal contracts fund nearly 25 percent of the total R&D carried out by industry and are focused primarily on aircraft and missiles and communications equipment.

Tax credits

The federal tax code allows a tax credit of up to 20 percent to companies that invest in R&D above a certain threshold. The Tax Reform Act of 1986 added credits to industry for

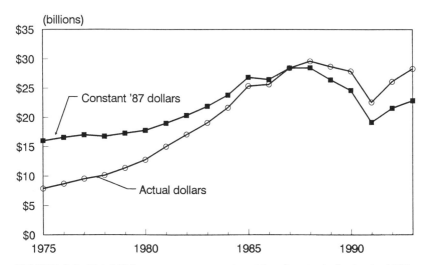

FIGURE 8.2. Total U.S. government contract funding to industry in 1993.
SOURCE: Data extracted from *Science and Engineering Indicators—1993*, p. 376.

research grants, contributions, and contracts awarded to universities and other nonprofit organizations. In 1994, the total tax credits to industry totaled $300M.

*Small business innovation
research (SBIR) program*

Eleven federal agencies participate in this program, and provide awards totaling close to $500M annually to small businesses. Through this program, qualified organizations can receive a phase-I research award of $50K to evaluate the technical and scientific merits of a new product concept and up to $500K in phase II to further develop it. The General Accounting Office reports that through the end of 1993, the SBIR program has produced approximately $3B in incremental sales revenue from SBIR recipients.

*Independent research and
development (IR&D) program*

This program allows industrial defense suppliers to obtain federal funds for R&D performed voluntarily in anticipation of government space and defense needs. Partial reimbursement of such expenses is credited to subsequent federal contracts. In 1992, the government reimbursed industry to the tune of $2.3B, or 48 percent of the total IR&D expenses incurred.

Defense conversion

Here, government defense funding is being used to smooth the transition of defense-dependent industries to commercial and civilian activities. This initiative totaled $1.3B in 1993, the largest segment of which was the Technology Reinvestment Project (TRP). Awards totaling $500M given from ARPA were awarded to industry-university-government teams for R&D in dual-use (military and commercial) technologies. Its purpose was to bolster the economic competitiveness of defense-dependent sources and increase the availability of defense technologies to the commercial sector. More than 2,800 proposals were submitted for 1993 funding, with four to five different organizations on-average participating on each proposal.

To be considered seriously for a TRP award, each proposed activity had to include:

- Participation from several different industry, university, nonprofit, and state and local government organizations.

- At least 50 percent cost sharing with the government.

Federal laboratories

There are approximately 700 federal laboratories, with a 1993 operating budget of $16.6B. The R&D carried out here is approximately 50 percent defense and 50 percent non-defense. Much of the defense-oriented R&D is conducted at the National Weapons Labs at Sandia, Los Alamos, and Lawrence Livermore. As the need for defense R&D in National Laboratories began decreasing in the mid-to-late '80s, the focus of the labs has begun to shift from defense to commercial (or dual-use) support. The Federal Technology Transfer Act of 1986 authorized the National Labs to enter into CRADAs (Cooperative Research and Development Agreements) with private industry, so that each could leverage the technical assistance of the other. As a result, the number of CRADAs grew from 108 in 1987 to 975 in 1991 and is continuing to grow as U.S. National Laboratories increasingly search for nondefense activities. More than 250 licensing agreements were made with industry in 1991, many as outgrowths of the CRADA activities.

Although each of the programs described above benefits some subset of industry, in total they represent fairly broad support for industry in its transition from defense-driven R&D to that needed to retain leadership in the global, commercial marketplace.

INDUSTRY-UNIVERSITY
PARTNERSHIPS

Collaboration between industry and universities also has increased significantly over the past several years. Once regarded as ivory towers, universities are now beginning to proactively seek industry partnerships—along with the bruises and scratches that accompany them. Interactions between industry technologists and university researchers bring several advantages to both parties. Industry receives:

- Access to leading-edge research—usually at modest cost.

- Access to students for potential employment.

- An opportunity to enhance the basic knowledge of their engineering staff.

Universities receive:

- A source of funding.

- Access to state-of-the-art industrial facilities.

- Special educational opportunities for their students.

- An opportunity to complement the knowledge of their faculty with practical tools and values.

- An opportunity to see their research usefully applied.

In general, universities have become much more proactive in seeking industry funding as federal defense support has slowed. One major change that has occurred over the past decade is the widespread formation of university centers or industrial affiliate programs. Such programs serve as mini-consortia, usually in a specific technology or applications area; they often involve 5 to 20 faculty members with their associated graduate students and provide focused research to a group of industrial clients. More often than not, they leverage their client's revenue with federal contracts for related R&D. Most major college departments have a few such centers, so that a single university may house 10 to 20 of them—primarily in science and engineering areas. By 1990, more than 1,000 such research centers had been formed in the United States. Since then, the number has increased even more.[8] Their work is predominantly basic and applied research, mixed with a small amount of short-term development projects.

There are several reasons for the dramatic increase in university centers:

- The reduction in federal defense contracts has encouraged faculty to actively seek industry funding. Banding together, faculty can illustrate sufficient mass and scale in a specific area to attract sponsorship.

- The federal agencies that do fund universities are often seeking an arrangement that can bring a project to practical completion. By combining forces with industry, a university can offer not only R&D, but also production and marketing of any resulting products.

- State and local governments often contribute to the centers to promote high-technology economic growth in their communities.

As evidence of the growing degree of collaboration, industry funding to U.S. colleges and universities has grown from $400M in 1983 to $1.5B in 1993.[9] Even when taking inflation into account, this represents a 10 percent annual growth rate in constant dollars!

However, collaboration between industry and universities is not easy because of their very different cultures and

---

[8]W. Cohen, R. Florida, and W.R. Goe, *University Industry Research Centers in the United States: Final Report to the Ford Foundation* (Carnegie Mellon University, Pittsburgh, 1993).

[9]*Science and Engineering Indicators—1993*, op. cit., p. 331.

objectives. Some of the major differences between their R&D methods are discussed in chapter 11.

INDUSTRY-INDUSTRY PARTNERSHIPS

Domestic consortia and alliances

Alliances in the United States have become commonplace, as company after company tries to leverage its capabilities and bolster its shortcomings in the marketplace. For example:

- Hewlett Packard joined Intel in an alliance to co-develop an advanced microprocessor, hopefully to thwart the effectiveness of IBM-Motorola-Apple's PowerPC chip.

- ITT joined Cablevision in a joint venture to purchase Madison Square Garden.

- The defense industry reeled from the acquisition of IBM's Federal Systems Division by Loral, GE's Aerospace Division by Martin Marietta, and Grumman by Northrup.

- Ford, Chrysler, and GM joined forces in a precompetitive consortia aimed at advanced automobile technologies.

Alliances take on many shapes, ranging from technology exchanges to outright acquisitions. In order of increasing complexity, the following types of relationships can be established:

- Mutual technology exchanges.

- Preferred vendor or supplier agreements.

- Foundry (manufacturing) agreements.

- Technology or product licensing.

- Research consortia.

- Technology or product co-development.

- Expanding product portfolios with partner's parts.

- Joint product or market development.

- Joint ventures.

- Mergers.

- Acquisitions.

Regarding research consortia, the National Cooperative Research Act of 1984 allows joint R&D cooperation between competitors without automatic liability for antitrust action. Through June 1993, more than 350 filings have been made of U.S. cooperative research ventures, with the rate increasing steadily over the past eight years (see Figure 8.3).[10]

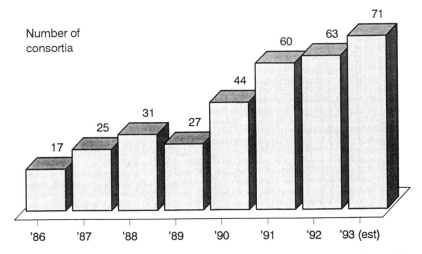

FIGURE 8.3. Number of U.S. cooperative research ventures registered in the United States since 1986.

---

[10]ibid., p. 122.

Many of the consortia are in regulated utility industries, such as electric power, gas and oil, and telecommunications; however, the act has also encouraged about an equal number of generic, precompetitive research consortia in industries as diverse as software, semiconductors, automobiles, textiles, food, sensors, and forest products. Examples of such consortia are listed in Table 8.4.

TABLE 8.4. A sample listing of U.S. research
and development consortia.

Organization	Membership
American Textile Partnership	Textile and apparel
Bellcore	Telecommunications
Electric Power Research Institute (EPRI)	Energy generation and distribution
Gas Research Institute (GRI)	Gas production and distribution
Great Lakes Composite Consortium	Manufacturing
Institute of Paper Science and Technology (IPST)	Pulp and paper products
International Life Sciences Institute (ILSI)	Food processing and distribution
Microelectronics and Computer Technology Corporation (MCC)	Computer and semiconductors
National Center for Manufacturing Sciences (NCMS)	Manufacturing
Ohio Aerospace Institute	Aerospace
Petroleum Industry Environmental Research Fund	Petroleum production and refining
Sematech	Semiconductor manufacturing
Semiconductor Research Corporation (SRC)	Semiconductor research
Software Productivity Consortium (SPC)	Software
U.S. Council for Automotive Research (USCAR)	Automobile manufacturers

SOURCE: Information provided through the courtesy of Strategic Analysis, Inc., Research Triangle Park, NC.

In the current environment, part of the new paradigm for technology development involves effective participation in research consortia and strategic technology alliances. In this regard, the following principles may be useful:

- Participation in consortia and the formation of technology alliances should be viewed as a natural, cost-effective way to meet product needs by acquiring new technology, rather than by finding products or markets to use limited existing technologies.

- Participation in alliances or consortia requires a major effort. Not surprisingly, the benefits of such an arrangement are directly proportional to the efforts applied. It is usually far better not to participate at all, than to apply a casual, low-priority effort; the latter approach is almost certain to generate disappointment and frustration by all participants. Effective participation requires:

  — Top-level management support.
  — A dedicated program manager to direct and coordinate the alliance or consortia activities and to distribute its results to appropriate personnel.
  — A budget sufficient to cover the necessary travel associated with vigorous participation.
  — A significant amount of company hardening or commercialization of any technology transferred from a consortium. This may not be ideal, but it is realistic.

Management of external R&D is more difficult than that of in-house programs because of the many barriers that exist between different companies, business cultures, and geographical locations. The single most important factor in attempting to manage alliances between different companies is that the expectations of the alliance be thoroughly defined and articulated in advance. Such expectations should cover all major elements of the working relationship, including product requirements, resource commitments, metrics, communication techniques, and most important—the personal responsibilities and commitments of the major participants.

International alliances

The number of international R&D alliances has also grown dramatically over the past several years. International alliances are usually much more difficult to initiate and implement than domestic ones because of major cultural and language differences as well as possible government restrictions. International alliances with U.S. industrial companies generally fall into either of the following two categories:

- *Manufacturing relationship.* The product design and marketing network of the U.S. company complements the manufacturing capabilities and capital investment of the foreign firm—usually from the Pacific Rim.

- *Product or marketing relationship.* A new product or technology is jointly developed (and perhaps jointly manufactured), but each organization retains exclusive marketing rights in its own country.

The largest number of international alliances for U.S. industry have thus far been with European companies—presumably because language and cultural issues are somewhat smaller for a U.S. company there than they would be for an alliance partner from the Far East. However, alliances with Japanese, Korean, and Chinese companies are indeed growing rapidly—in part because of the technical prowess of the Pacific Rim, and in part to the large potential market there.

IN SUMMARY

Over the past few years, the U.S. government has begun implementing a *de facto* technology policy that attempts to provide a transition for defense-dependent businesses into the commercial arena, while attempting to promote effective collaboration among industry, government, and academic organizations, especially in certain critical high-tech industries. Several legislative acts and tax code revisions have been initiated for these purposes.

Technology collaboration can take many forms. For industry technologists, a make or buy decision should be exercised for upcoming development requirements, with potential assistance available from universities, R&D centers, National Laboratories, or private industry. Technology development and the selection of a technology source should be driven by product requirements—not determine them.

Effective participation in external alliances and consortia is essential to acquire leveraged technology to meet product or market needs. However, managing alliances and consortia is more difficult than managing internal programs because of the diversity of interests, culture, geography, and language.

CHAPTER 9

The Vision

> It is change, continuing change, inevitable change, that is
> the dominant factor in society today. No sensible deci-
> sion can be made any longer without taking into account
> not only the world as it is, but the world as it will be.
> —Isaac Asimov, 1978

Change is indeed inevitable—in life and in business.
Thinking (hoping, wishing, planning) that tomorrow will
be as today is a delusion. For only briefly do business for-
tunes remain steady—usually they are either growing or
decaying. In fact, even a stable business environment is
generally comprised of a set of expanding and contracting
activities—the sum of which may be approximately constant for a relatively short period of time. From such a perspective, there is only one reasonable alternative: to em-
brace change head-on at all times and to make every
possible attempt to put it to your best advantage.

Most technology-oriented organizations acknowledge
the need for change (growth) through a vision statement
that addresses the future directions for the organization. A
vision statement should primarily reflect the big picture
(doing the right things), but it should also briefly capture
the major principles used to execute the strategic plan

(doing things right). For example, a vision statement for two different types of product organizations (X and Y) might read as follows:

- To become one of the largest international suppliers of product X through world-class, cost-effective manufacturing capabilities and strong partnerships with valued international sales distributors.

- To become a preferred U.S. supplier of product Y through the rapid development of high-quality, leading-edge products that continuously meet or exceed the needs of our customers.

The first statement might apply to high-volume commodity products such as memory chips, consumer electronic products, standard lumber, appliances, and low-cost clothing. The second would be more appropriate for high-performance products, such as large-capacity disk drives, laser-printer engines, and high-fashion apparel. Of course, in both cases, other planning documents within the organization would address the specifics of achieving the vision.

A VISION FOR THE NEW DEVELOPMENT PARADIGM

In the previous four chapters, we have discussed several important elements of the new development paradigm that is being embraced throughout U.S. technology-based industries. In this section, we summarize that process in two simple charts that are intended to serve as part of an organization's development vision. They do not address the specifics of a single type of product, for that will vary from company to company and from product to product. But they do describe a common foundation that should apply to nearly all sophisticated products.

The elements of the vision included in Table 9.1 describe an ideal process, carried out by a highly interactive

TABLE 9.1. Our Vision

The people

1. Multifunctional, self-directed work teams are employed for concurrent product or technology development. The teams are empowered by management for tactical completion of the program.

2. The work team includes major customers and suppliers (internal or external), especially in the definition stage.

3. Managers supply a clear description of the program mission, including cost, or performance requirements; they also facilitate program needs as they occur.

The process

1. A formal, written guide describes the product or technology development process. It includes detailed expectations for the five major phases:

   - Advanced planning.
   - Definition.
   - Design.
   - Demonstration.
   - Customer support.

2. The process includes significant up-front efforts in advanced planning and definition to analyze cost-effective options to meet market and customer needs. It requires a business plan with financial expectations as well as long- and short-term opportunities and risks.

3. The process has strategic management reviews at only a few selected gates. Here, program can-

TABLE 9.1. Our Vision (continued)

cellation or redefinition is seriously considered upon reaching major obstacles to the original mission.

4. The design process includes not only environmental parameters, but also manufacturing and test variability. It attempts to statistically center the design with respect to these variables (design for manufacturability and design for test).

5. Enabling technologies are driven by product needs. They are developed internally or acquired externally to meet such requirements. Collaborative external R&D is nurtured through alliances or consortia to leverage investments.

6. The development process itself is considered an important internal product and is the subject of continuous improvement efforts.

Methods and tools

1. Total quality management (TQM) principles based on customer satisfaction are applied to product and technology development. Continuous improvement of the development process is sought through activities such as benchmarking, process characterization, and activity-based cost accounting.

2. Quality function deployment (QFD) and an analysis of product design options are used to best fit product features to customer requirements.

3. When CAD tools are widely used, a library of design modules is established for subsequent reuse.

4. A culture is established to promote innovation in product and technology development. The objective of such a program is to capture novel approaches and product concepts from all sources, including employees and (especially) customers.

Metrics

1. Metrics are established for three different purposes:

   - Strategic assessment of active and completed programs.
   - Tactical assessment of active programs.
   - Benchmarking with other companies.

2. The metrics useed to track active programs are established to monitor progress against expectations:

   - The metrics are chosen to capture only the most essential factors and do so with minimum data and organizational disruption.
   - The metrics are defined so that their graphic presentation easily conveys relative progress.
   - They are standardized over all similar departments within the organization.
   - The metrics are reviewed regularly and used to guide improvements.

employee work team. Our vision is intended to be visionary only in the intensity and totality to which these attributes are pursued. However, all of the attributes are based on practical approaches currently being implemented for product and technology development throughout U.S. industry. The statements contained in the vision describe methods that are employed, in part, by nearly all companies; yet they are used effectively, in their entirety, by none.

IN SUMMARY

Change in the business world is inevitable; it is to be confronted and embraced in a quest to make tomorrow's directions and methods better than today's. An organization's vision statement should indicate the purpose and directions for the organization's future as well as the methods through which they will be achieved.

In this chapter, a table is presented that provides the basis for developing a vision for an organization embracing the new development paradigm. It contains the elements that describe the people, the process, the methods, and the metrics for building the right things right.

CHAPTER 10

Industry

Effectiveness

LARGE VERSUS SMALL COMPANIES

The new development process—whether for product or
technology development—has some elements that are familiar to U.S. engineers and others that are foreign to
nearly everything our engineers and managers have experienced. For example, U.S. leaders have traditionally
been strong on action and weak on planning. Hence, they
are more at ease with prototyping than with advanced
planning or product definition. Similarly, our strong incli-
nation toward individual accomplishment makes work
team dynamics less natural for us than it is for Pacific
Rim engineers, whose culture is steeped in building consensus.

Certain types of companies also find the new development paradigm to be more natural (and effective) than others. For example, it becomes apparent that different size
companies would have significantly different product and
technology development capabilities, as discussed further
throughout this chapter. For convenience, we treat three
categories of companies, based on size and breadth of market focus:

1. Small companies.

2. Large corporations with a relatively narrow product focus. One example of such a company is Intel, the large U.S. merchant semiconductor company with a strong microprocessor and memory product focus for computer applications. Others might include the big-three U.S. automakers, Sun Microsystems, and U.S. Steel.

3. Large corporations with a broad portfolio of products. Hewlett Packard and Motorola are examples in the electronics industry, each of which may provide tens of thousands of different electronic products. General Mills has a similarly broad product portfolio related to the food industry.

Large U.S. corporations, in general, have been struggling desperately in their effort to become or remain globally competitive. During 1993, *Business Week* reported that over a five-year period, large companies (with 500 or more employees) recorded a net loss of 2.3 million jobs, while small companies provided most of the 5.8 million new ones. Throughout the remainder of 1993, large corporations are expected to slash another 300,000 jobs, while small companies will need another 1.7 million new employees.[1]

The rapid pace of new technology introductions has reduced the importance of corporate size and manufacturing economies of scale. Today's successful companies are flexible, creative, close to the customer, and quick to market.

> "Get that small-company soul—and small company speed—inside our big-company body."[2]
> —*Jack Welch, CEO, General Electric*

[1] J. A. Byrne, "Enterprise," *Business Week*, Special Issue—Enterprise 93, p. 12, October 1993.

[2] ibid.

Some of the specific strengths and weaknesses of different-size companies are discussed in the following sections.

Small companies

A small company usually has a limited product line, and perhaps a few hundred employees. Consequently, most of the development engineers know the company's strategic directions, its products, and a large fraction of their co-workers. They also know the company's few major customers, and probably the general directions of its customers' products. This scenario considerably enhances both the planning and implementation tasks that comprise the overall development cycle. Planning is straight forward because nearly all of the employees are continually thinking about such opportunities during the course of their work. Similarly, small organizations are too lean to have organizational bureaucracies and geographically-scattered operations. Consequently, transfers between development engineering, manufacturing, quality, and sales organizations are usually informal events among people who have been working together on the project all along.

However, one potential problem is the limited commitment a small company might receive from potential customers, who consider its size too risky to justify extensive collaboration during product definition. In addition, limited capital resources can restrict demonstration and production capabilities. In such cases, the company's dependence on external assembly and test resources can delay product completion. Product support for external manufacturing organizations can also be difficult, since manufacturing expertise in small product-oriented companies is usually thin.

Large, broad-market companies

Such companies struggle in nearly all of the phases of the development process because of the complications that come with large size and a broad charter. Consider the following problems:

- Bureaucracies.

- Company facilities that are geographically separated.

- Separate departments for quality, engineering, manufacturing, sales, and marketing.

- Employee team members who haven't worked together previously and who may not even know each other.

- Multiple product lines competing for the same resources.

Advanced planning and product definition are difficult because of the diversity of customers, applications, and market segments that apply to a broad product portfolio. Technology and manufacturing roadmaps are similarly complex. For reasons that are more traditional than rational, many large U.S. corporations also seem to have very limited strategic or advanced planning activities; those responsibilities are often left to divisional general managers, who already have their plates full with day-to-day operations. As a result of such complexities, advanced planning is often poorly done. The frequency of such planning is also usually limited to once a year—just in time for the company's required strategic business plan. This plan, by the way, is often an executive-only exercise that is not disseminated throughout the organization, and is filed away (for next year) soon after the required corporate presentation.

*Large company
with narrow market*

In many ways, such companies have the best of both worlds. On the one hand, they are sufficiently narrow to know their markets and customers very well and to have all of the corporate resources focused in a single direction; they also are sufficiently large to have adequate resources to properly support development and to be taken seriously by their customers. Companies like Microsoft or Intel are hard to beat—they are good at what they do, and strong enough to tackle just about any product opportunity in their field. Advanced planning and product definition in such companies should be relatively straightforward.

There is only one fundamental concern for large companies with a narrow focus: their size still presents serious difficulties in dealing with complex organizations and procedures, distant factories, and employees who are unfamiliar with each other. Employee communications are not much easier here than in large companies with a broad product portfolio. These are among the most challenging difficulties that faces all growing companies as they attempt to make the transition from small (<$50M) to mid-size—and the reason that so many small companies never get larger.

The vast technical, manufacturing, and application capabilities of large U.S. companies (with either a broad- or narrow-market focus) do provide certain advantages for prototyping and production support. In these areas, adequate hardware, software, and personnel are available to drive the product-to-market process. However, the complexity of these resources is also a serious obstacle, with multiple worldwide manufacturing sites, impenetrable business information systems, and centralized functional organizations. These complexities hamper communications, add bureaucratic delays, and generally frustrate technical progress. In such a climate, product development is often handled by champions, who through their persistence, assertiveness, creativity, and experience are able to penetrate such barriers. Fortunately, the unavoidable variability of this approach is beginning to be recognized, and development programs like the ones in this book are now being embraced. Clearly, an organization such as this has the most to gain by establishing a simplified development process and a concurrent methodology.

In Tables 10.1 through 10.3, we provide a summary assessment of the strengths and weaknesses that the three selected types of companies are thought to have in carrying out the five phases of product and technology development.

It is important to note that the assessments in Tables 10.1 through 10.3 do not represent any specific companies. Rather, they are meant to represent the inherent degree of difficulty that one type of company is apt to have with respect to the other types of companies in each category.

In Table 10.4, we summarize the characteristics of the same company categories with respect to four attributes that facilitate new product and technology development. Although customer involvement is limited throughout industry, a large company with diverse product and technology portfolios is particularly handicapped in its ability to be close to a wide range of customers and application areas.

ASSESSING THE NEW DEVELOPMENT PARADIGM IN YOUR COMPANY

An appraisal chart to help determine the current status of product or technology development in a specific organization is provided in Table 10.5. Here, each of 22 attributes of the new development paradigm is rated on the basis of 1 (poor) to 5 (excellent), and the responses totaled. Most U.S. companies would be expected to score in the 65 range, representing an average response of 3 for each query. Such scores are consistent with the assessment that most companies are involved in the paradigm shift, but primarily in the formative stages. Confusion and false starts are nearly as frequent as major victories. But this is not unexpected

TABLE 10.1. Potential strengths and weaknesses of product or technology development in large companies with a relatively broad product portfolio.

Phase	Strengths	Weaknesses
Advanced planning		• Planning is a second priority to operational issues. • Insufficient resources are assigned to planning. • Technology and product family roadmaps are complex and broad.
Definition		• Customer involvement is insufficient. • Products are driven more by technology than by market. • Market and financial analysis before commitment is insufficient. • Inadequate resources are committed to approved projects.
Design	• Good design tools and systems. • CAD has received industry focus to handle product complexity.	• Design is not sufficiently sensitive to manufacturing and test variations and to qualification requirements.
Demonstration	• Adequate resources in all areas of manufacturing	• Organizational complexity and multiple international manufacturing sites create undesirable barriers. • Barriers between separate manufacturing and development organizations.
Customer support		• Development responsibility is viewed to be finished when the product is introduced into manufacturing.

TABLE 10.2. Potential effectiveness of product or technology development in large companies with a narrow product portfolio.

Phase	Strengths	Weaknesses
Advanced planning	• Roadmaps are well defined because of the limited number of standard product families. • Limited number of product families are recognized as high priority.	
Definition	• Customers and their needs are well known. • Limited number of standard products with large volumes allows precise definition.	
Design	• Good design tools and systems. • CAD has received industry focus to handle product complexity.	• Design is not sufficiently sensitive to manufacturing and test variations and to qualification requirements.
Demonstration	• Adequate resources in all areas of manufacturing.	• Organizational complexity and multiple international manufacturing sites create undesirable barriers.
Customer support		• Barriers exist between separate manufacturing and development organizations. • Development responsibility viewed to be finished when product is introduced into manufacturing.

174

TABLE 10.3. Potential effectiveness of product or technology development in small companies.

Phase	Strengths	Weaknesses
Advanced planning	• Roadmaps are well defined because of limited size of product portfolio. • Directions of product families are recognized as high priority.	• Technology planning may have unknown problems due to dependence on external company's strategic directions.
Definition	• Customers and their needs are few and well known. • Product scope is sufficiently narrow to allow good definition.	• Company may not be large enough to be taken seriously by major customers.
Design		• Design is not sufficiently sensitive to manufacturing and test variations and to qualification requirements.
Demonstration		• Limited company resources. • Dependence on third-party manufacturing capabilities limits options. • Major barriers between separate manufacturing and development organizations (companies).
Customer support		• Little manufacturing skill to support production problems.

TABLE 10.4. Overview of product development characteristics
of different types of U.S. corporations.

	Small Company	Large Company— Broad Product Portfolio	Large Company— Narrow Product Portfolio
Knowledge of and collaboration with customer	Fair	Poor	Good
Sharp product or technology focus	Good	Poor	Good
Simple development process	Good	Poor	Fair
Resources or capital availability	Poor	Good	Good

when change is cultural and when it affects nearly all employees.

IN SUMMARY

Three types of organizations are described in this chapter:
large corporations with a broad or a narrow product focus
and small companies. A large corporation with a broad
product portfolio suffers the worst of both worlds: complexity and lack of focus. During the advanced planning
and definition phases, it is mired by the complexity of corporate product and technology roadmaps. Although it has
adequate resources to support the design and demonstration phases, it must struggle to overcome the multiple barriers within its vast organizational and geographical network.

A small company can plan better because of the limited
scope of its products and can execute better because of the
close personal interactions and communications that accompany its limited size. However, it struggles to be taken
seriously by its customers and must get by with far more
limited design and demonstration resources.

TABLE 10.5. An evaluation to assess the extent to which the new product or technology development paradigm has been implemented.

Formal development process	1 to 5

Formal development process
- Development process documented, widely distributed, and operational. ☐
- Engineers and managers trained in process implementation. ☐
- Continuous improvement efforts regularly applied to process. ☐
- Benchmarking used for enabling technologies. ☐

Advanced planning
- Mission and vision statements well understood and consistent with management actions. ☐
- 5+ year family roadmaps in place for major products. ☐
- 5+ year roadmaps in place for enabling technologies such as component processing, assembly, test, and design systems. ☐

Concurrent development teams
- Multifunctional work teams widely used for product and technology development. ☐
- Teams empowered by management for day-to-day activities. ☐
- Clear mission and boundary conditions communicated by management at program initiation. ☐

Definition
- Strong customer participation. ☐
- Product or technology benefits are analyzed against customer needs (QFD). ☐
- Business plan prepared before product development effort is approved. ☐
- Resource commitments tied to program development approval. ☐
- Target specifications clearly understood and communicated. ☐
- Plans for market launch established in business plan. Advertising and promotional costs included in development budget. ☐

Design and demonstration
- Broad design methodology employed (DFM, DFT). ☐
- Baseline data in place for development cycle times. ☐
- Schedule tracked regularly with standardized, company-wide metrics. ☐
- Management reviews only at critical decision gates. ☐
- Products terminated or redirected when original objectives cannot be met. ☐

Customer support
- Development team actively supports production yield enhancement efforts. ☐

1 – Not at all   2 – Hardly ever   3 – Sometimes   4 – Usually   5 – Almost always

Perhaps the optimal arrangement for product and technology development is found in a large organization having a narrow product portfolio. Here, planning, design, and demonstration activities need not struggle unreasonably with the complexities of very broad product or technology portfolios; yet the development organization usually has adequate resources and tools to master design, demonstration, and customer support requirements.

In any company of any size, empowered work teams, concurrent development, customer focus, process characterization, sensible metrics, and a comprehension of the five-phase development process will dramatically enhance the time-to-market and impact of its new products.

CHAPTER 11

The New
Paradigm in U.S.
Universities

Colleges and universities are important elements in the overall technical infrastructure of the United States. Its 3,600 institutions serve 14,000,000 students and annually provide approximately 2,000,000 degrees—about a quarter in science and engineering.[1] In such fields, the United States is viewed as having one of the best educational systems in the world, as evidenced by the fact that more than 30 percent of the engineering and math students in its graduate programs are from foreign countries![2] But being very good does not preclude improvement.

Most U.S. technical universities have at least two, and sometimes three, missions: education, research, and in some cases, local industrial support. In each of these, there is a need for change to support (and benefit from) the new development paradigm and the quality methods that accompany it. However, for the most part, the university system is far behind industry in embracing such change. According to Professor John E. Gibson, writing for the National Academy of Engineering:

---

[1] *Science and Engineering Indicators—1993,* op. cit., p. 39.

[2] ibid., p. 52.

"American business leaders are now well in advance of engineering and business schools in recognizing and practicing total quality principles, participative management, worker empowerment, and the like."[3]

At the 1991 Total Quality Forum in Cincinnati, keynote speaker Robert Kaplan, a professor of Harvard University's Graduate School of Business Administration, stated that:

"Fewer than five percent—and perhaps as little as one percent—of about six hundred U.S. business schools have been affected by the quality revolution that is driving U.S. businesses."[4]

Interestingly, the Harvard Business School is beginning to revamp its own curriculum to incorporate teamwork and integrated (rather than specialized) business instruction.[5]

Dr. Kaplan's views are also supported by the author's professional experience. In a 1993 survey of 130 professors working in semiconductor research, approximately 80 percent responded that there were no TQM programs in place in their departments—not in teaching, research, or administrative areas.[6]

In the following sections, we examine the new product and technology paradigm for each of the university's three major missions.

---

[3]J. E. Gibson, "Taylorism and Professional Education," *Foundations of World-Class Manufacturing Systems,* op. cit.

[4]B. Jorgensen, "Industry to Business Schools: Smarten Up to TQM or Else," *Electronic Business,* p. 85–90, Oct. 1992.

[5]"A Case Study in Change at Harvard," *Business Week,* p. 42, Nov. 1993.

[6]Private survey sponsored by the Semiconductor Research Corporation, Research Triangle Park, NC and conducted by the author.

UNIVERSITY RESEARCH

One unfortunate characteristic of the traditional university research program is its isolation from industry technology users—being driven largely by the technical expertise of the faculty and the educational needs of the students, and only secondarily by market or customer requirements. To some extent, this is necessary to support the university's instructional mission (without the short-term fluctuations of the business world) and to maintain narrow pockets of world-class technical expertise. However, with declining engineering enrollments, tight education budgets, and shrinking defense funding, universities are coming under increasing pressure to pursue incremental sources of revenue, including industry funding. This unavoidably translates to shorter-term, more relevant research. It also requires that the cycle time of the university research process be shortened.

These objectives can be pursued by extending the generic five-phase development process described in chapters 5 and 6 to university applied research. For such projects, the process has only slightly different descriptors, as summarized in Table 11.1. For example, a university proposal for a research contract is equivalent to industry product definition; experimental prototypes are analogous to low-volume factory runs in industry, and so forth. Several other useful analogies are indicated in Table 11.2. For example, university applied research projects do have customers—specifically the funding sponsor and the intended end user. It is the program manager's (i.e., the principal investigator's) responsibility to see that each of these is satisfied with the research and its results.

It is especially important to recognize that the process described in Table 11.1 is dynamic. Project goals and directions should change in the light of experimental observations or new insights. In fact, an additional discovery opportunity must be added within the demonstration phase

TABLE 11.1. Five-phase model for university applied research projects.

Phase	Research Activities
Advanced planning:	Assessing the technology's strategic directions and long-range industry and government needs. Translating this information into a personal set of long-range research goals.
Definition:	Defining the specific research objectives and the approach. Identifying all resource requirements and timing for major research milestones. Determining collaborative partnerships. Writing a proposal for funding.
Design:	Determining the specific architecture, test structures, and procedures that will be used to implement the research project.
Demonstration:	Preparing technology prototypes. Exploring performance and dependencies. Evaluating the resulting capabilities against agreed-upon criteria. Discovering new effects or behavior.
Customer support (technology transfer):	Documenting results in manuals or professional publications. Refining the technology or product to meet end-user applications. Troubleshooting customer start-up problems.

TABLE 11.2. Analogous activities between university applied research projects and industry product development.

University activity	Industry analogy
• Formal research proposal	• Product definition; business plan
• Student defense of thesis plan	• Design review
• Principal investigator	• Program manager
• Funding agency	• Customer 1
• Industry end user	• Customer 2
• Experimental prototypes	• Low-volume production runs for evaluation samples
• Evaluation of final prototypes for thesis and journal publication	• Product qualification tests
• Transfer to industry end user	• Sale to customer

for university research, as shown in Figure 11.1. Here, new insights (discovery) might lead to any one of several project modifications:

- If new or *additional data* is needed, no project redirections are called for, and the university team must simply repeat a portion of the demonstration phase.

- If a *different kind of data or a new approach* is needed, the project must revert to the design phase, where a new set of experimental conditions must be established.

- If a *completely new direction is required*, the project must revert to the definition phase; a major redirection should then be discussed or negotiated with the customers. There is no reason a new direction shouldn't be pursued vigorously; however, abandonment of the original direction may adversely affect the plans of the

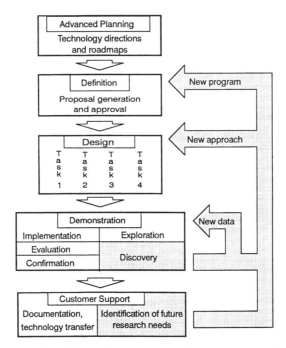

FIGURE 11.1. A revised five-phase process that portrays a discovery activity in basic or exploratory research.

customer or the funding agency—and therefore should not be treated casually.

> It is better to have a plan and change it, than to have no plan at all.

It is intellectually fashionable to argue that university research is too basic to fit an organized process model like the one shown in Figure 11.1. But an increasing number of projects in leading U.S. technical universities are in fact quite applied—as evidenced by the university community's widespread push to attract sponsors for their centers and industrial affiliate programs and by their pursuit of government and industrial research contracts. For nearly all such contracts, a formal proposal that captures many of the elements of the research process is required and accepted as standard practice. Unfortunately, the use of these proposals is often limited to pre-contract funding evaluation—and set aside by both researchers and sponsors once the contract is awarded.

In a 1993 survey, 130 research faculty were asked to consider their applied research projects from the perspective of the research model described in Table 11.1. Interestingly, 96 percent of the respondents were able to do so, providing specific estimates of the time they (and their students) devoted to each phase. The results, shown in Figure 11.2 speak well for the distribution of total efforts across the entire breadth of the project—and in fact, are quite representative of a typical industry distribution across the same phases. They also demonstrate that applied research projects in U.S. universities can be represented by the process model proposed throughout this book.

We also must recognize that some fraction of university research (even applied research) proceeds not by plan, but through unplanned creative insights. Admittedly, the process described in Figure 11.1 does not take such creativ-

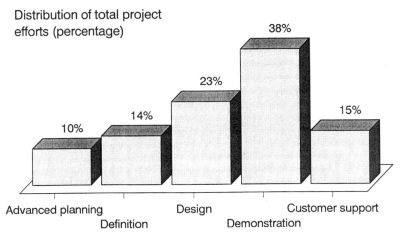

Distribution of total project efforts (percentage)

Advanced planning   Design   Customer support
       Definition   Demonstration

FIGURE 11.2. Distribution of efforts in each development phase across a set of applied university research projects.
(Responses are from 130 faculty representing 45 different U.S. technical universities.)
SOURCE: Data provided through the courtesy of the Semiconductor Research Corporation, Research Triangle Park, NC.

ity into consideration—nor will any other organized process description. Such occurrences should be recognized not by eliminating the need for organization, discipline, and project management in most applied research activities, but by allowing a reasonable amount of slack time in professors' schedules—time to wander and think and stimulate creativity. The balance between organized R&D projects and creative brainstorming should vary between disciplines, departments, and individual professors, and university management must be challenged to find and maintain the right balance. The United States has perhaps the finest university research system in the world, and it is essential that its activities remain balanced not only with respect to managed versus creative research, but also with respect to its multiple responsibilities in teaching, research, and community support. However, the need for balance should not endorse isolation from the general customer base, nor should it discourage discipline in applied research methodology.

In my opinion, there are four areas of the university research model that are weak from a technology development perspective: customer participation, student training, customer support, and marketing. These are discussed in the following sections.

Customer participation

In the advanced planning and definition phases of R&D, extensive interactions are required with potential technology customers. In the case of funded university research programs, there are often two customers—the funding sponsor and the commercial or government user. Although the top-level requirements of the funding agency are usually stated during a formal proposal process, the ultimate success (and value) of the program lies in understanding the needs of the end users. Unfortunately, despite efforts by all parties, the interaction of potential end users on university programs is limited, and multiyear research programs that lack technological relevance are consequently initiated.

The lack of sufficient customer participation in the advanced planning and definition phases is not solely the fault of the academic community. It is amplified by the difficulty in obtaining the sustained support and interest of industry colleagues due to their short-term business priorities and their indifference to long-term, high-risk university activities. Despite the difficulties in implementing such involvement, it is absolutely essential to do so. Many approaches have been tried—some more successfully than others. One program, initiated by the Semiconductor Research Corporation on behalf of its industry consortium members, has established a mentor program, in which one-on-one industry-professor relationships are set up in areas of mutual technology interest.[7] This program has received considerable success, as evidenced by its 450 participating

---

[7]The Semiconductor Research Corporation is a not-for-profit consortium that serves the research needs of the North American semiconductor industry. It is located in Research Triangle Park, NC.

mentors. Its major effectiveness stems from the working-level relationships that are built over several years between faculty, students, and industry technologists.

Executive-level collaboration between university and industry leaders can also be helpful, since it can address strategic needs and responsibilities. These usually occur via industry positions on university advisory boards. However, in general, there is far too little collaboration of any kind—to the detriment of the overall effectiveness of the university research process and its end users.

Student training

As indicated earlier, the distribution of personnel across the five phases of the research process is quite reasonable (recall Figure 11.2). However, the distribution of students and faculty individually provides quite a different conclusion. As illustrated in Figure 11.3, professors are found to allocate their time quite evenly across the process; however, graduate students participate almost exclusively in the back end

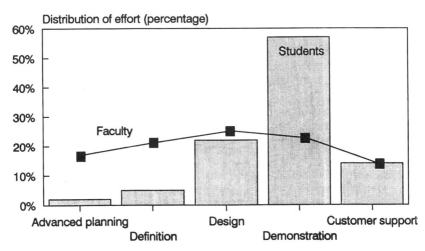

FIGURE 11.3. Percentage of student and faculty time spent on each phase of a university applied research project.
SOURCE: Data provided through the courtesy of the Semiconductor Research Corporation, Research Triangle Park, NC.

of the process—especially in the demonstration phase. Such a distribution is not surprising for two reasons:

- Research proposals are often submitted many months, perhaps even a year in advance of award. In many instances, the student who will carry out the work is not even associated with the professor that far in advance.

- In the first year or two of a graduate thesis, the student is usually not sufficiently experienced in his or her field to be able to plan the future direction of the research.

For both reasons, faculty members carry out nearly all of the advanced planning and definition activities.

The danger with this scenario is that the graduate students may not adequately appreciate the critical importance of front-end planning and definition activities. Upon graduation, the student takes the same perspective to his or her employment, where strategic up-front planning is probably insufficient to begin with.

A second shortcoming is in the lack of student training in the research process itself. Despite faculty verbalization of the importance of student training in the research process, a very small fraction (no more than 10 percent to 15 percent) have any written process description or material to aid their training.

Customer support

Another area that requires change in the university research process is the final support phase. For a research program, this translates to a transition into the customer's research, engineering, or manufacturing organization. More attention is now being paid to this in programs that are directly funded by industry. However, it is still a weak link in the research and development chain, due to the necessary student turnover and the disinclination of academic researchers toward documentation or industrial implementation.

One of the more successful technology transfer approaches is the recruitment of a graduate student by industry, followed by an initial assignment to transfer his or her university research into that company. However, this is costly as a generic solution to transfer research and limited by the number of graduating students hired by a particular company. A more satisfying solution builds customer involvement throughout the research program so that the transfer is a natural consequence of the work team's efforts (much like an industrial transfer from the product development team to the manufacturing and sales organizations).

One unusual approach to university-industry technology transfer has been proposed by Kovacs and Augustine.[8] They recommend that highly qualified senior industry engineers be jointly recruited for a three-year university professorship. In this plan, the goal of the industry professor would be to teach 50 percent and to promote technology exchange between university and industry the other 50 percent. This approach would reduce the isolation of the university from industry, while inserting university technology into the industry organization. A side benefit for the industry professor would be to recharge him or her with an understanding and appreciation of the principles of his or her field from an academic perspective. As proposed, the cost of the program would be shared by industry, university and government (in the form of tax credits).

The word *relevancy* rarely appears in university research contracts. And yet, it should be highlighted as a differentiating theme, much as technical eminence is today. Research contracts should be based on customer satisfaction, with increasingly demanding requirements for technology transfer in each year of a typical three-year program. Milestones need to be added that require commitments for technology insertion as a requisite for funding renewal. In short, best

---

[8]M. G. Kovacs and N. R. Augustine, "Industrial Professorships: Enhancing Technology Transfer and U.S. Engineering Education," p. 24–27, PRISM, April 1992.

efforts should be replaced with specific action for continuation. The risk, of course, is micromanagement and short-term focus; however, a few steps in that direction would probably be useful.

The subject of expectations should also be addressed here, for unexpressed expectations between organizations as different as universities and industry are the principal cause of disappointment and ineffectiveness in any collaboration between them. Figure 11.4 lists topics that should be frankly discussed and resolved early in any collaboration. From a technical standpoint, equipment interfaces and software formats can be easily accommodated when planned in advance; alternate reconfigurations at the time of transfer can be considerably more difficult. Resource availability can also have a serious impact on the transfer schedule, and commitments regarding the schedule and level of resources must be known ahead of time. Most important, the personal expectations each worker has of his or

Different cultures and paradigms require a clear understanding between the organizations:

- Technical needs versus capabilities
- Product definition
- Specific timing, features, limitations for deliverables
- Resources available
- Personal responsibilities, limitations, and commitments
- Personal motivation and expectations
- Frequency and means of regular interactions

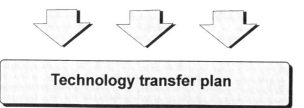

Technology transfer plan

FIGURE 11.4. Expectations that should be addressed by university and industry personnel working on a collaborative R&D project.

her partner can dramatically affect the nature of their inter-actions, and make the overall transfer shaky or smooth.

All considerations such as these, should be formally ad-dressed in a technology transfer plan for the collaboration. This will help ensure that the expected technology will be transferred from university to industry based on the agreed-upon expectations and commitments of both parties.

Marketing research

The marketing function occurs throughout most of the phases of the development cycle for commercial products and should not be ignored for research and technology de-velopment. Today, university research is usually marketed by the principal investigator of the project. Such an indi-vidual is highly technical but usually naive in business or commercial relevance. Moreover, the principal investigator is immersed in technical details and often finds it difficult to highlight the big picture for an interested listener.

> All I wanted to know was the time—not how the watch works.[9]

An important capability for reviews with a potential customer or funding sponsor is that of providing a brief and understandable overview of the program status and its potential impact. Although elementary, many researchers are unable to accomplish it. A valuable exercise for any uni-versity researcher would be to develop a brief summary of his or her program—one that includes:

- The problem (why do this research?).

- The approach.

---

[9]Origin unknown, but often quoted by Jon E. Cornell, former President, Harris Semiconductor, Melbourne, FL.

- The major highlight of the project to date.

- Future plans.

- Potential impact.

Despite the seemingly vast content in this simple list, a successful research leader can provide an interesting and enthusiastic message hitting each of these subjects in just one or two minutes. The most important topics on the list are the first and last. Without an appreciation for the problem and the potential impact, all other details are academic. An interesting one-minute message can be applied in any setting—at a lunch table or a conference table.

> Most researchers don't consider their work to be a product—and they must.

Faculty are generally not motivated by the market success of their resulting technology, but by the peer recognition achieved while carrying out the research. Such recognition comes primarily from publications, conference presentations, and the success of their graduate students— not from a project milestone. It's not the destination, but the journey that counts. This differs greatly from industry's tunnel vision toward the ever-shrinking market window for its products. It's not life or death—it's more important than that.

In the face of dropping engineering enrollments (a 13 percent reduction in engineering students in the past decade[10]), reduced defense budgets, and a general emphasis on technology alliances, university-industry partnerships will necessarily grow in importance and frequency. Collaboration so borne will be more customer focused and

---

[10]"Coming off the Drawing Board: Better Engineers," *Business Week*, p. 70, Aug. 2, 1993.

will gradually incorporate many of the techniques discussed throughout this book.

UNIVERSITY TECHNICAL CURRICULA

The U.S. technology work force poses a dichotomy in its job mix. On the one hand, we have companies that can't find the skilled workers they need to respond to business needs; and on the other, we have large numbers of unskilled workers who can't find decent jobs. Much of the responsibility for this dilemma is laid at the feet of the public school system. A growing number of our high school students are ill prepared for high-tech employment—usually placing near the bottom of international tests in math and science. It's not that our public schools haven't made progress, they have. For example, only 50 percent of all students completed high school in the '50s, while 80 percent do today.[11] But U.S. public schools have shorter academic years, less homework, and a broader social agenda than their global counterparts. According to Willard R. Daggett, director of the International Center for Leadership in Education, "they [American high schools] don't have a relevant curriculum for a technological information-based society."[12]

Our university educational programs struggle with similar problems. Quality, continuous improvement, innovation, and teamwork have now become the foundation of corporations that have achieved global competitiveness. Yet, the methods by which the contents of a four-year undergraduate engineering or science program are transferred to a student have changed little in the last 50 years. Despite the advent of sophisticated multimedia electronics and vast computer networks, the instructional material is still transferred primarily through personal lectures, complemented

---

[11]"Quality in Education: a New Collaborative Initiative, *FOCUS* (National Center for Manufacturing Sciences), p. 1, Aug. 1993.

[12]ibid.

by textbooks and daily homework assignments. Moreover, with a professor's career (including tenure) tied so closely to research and its funding, teaching advances often receive little attention from a large segment of the faculty. Most important for the new development paradigm, the focus is still primarily on individual learning and the content is restricted to traditional science and engineering.

There are two elements of such a program that leave a graduating student poorly prepared for important aspects of a career in industry:

- *Curricular content.* The absence of program management, communication, and basic financial tools and little or no exposure to quality methods.

- *Individual focus.* The strong individual focus discourages effective teamwork and collaboration.

Each of these is discussed in the following sections.

Curricular content

In recognition of the sophistication of today's high-tech products and systems as well as the pervasiveness of electronics throughout virtually all industrial activities significant progress has been made in integrating previously disparate curricula. In Berkeley, for example, a four-year undergraduate program called mechatronics has been developed to integrate mechanical and electrical engineering concepts.[13] At Carnegie-Mellon, differential calculus is being introduced into a new sophomore electrical engineering course. At the University of Pennsylvania's Wharton Business School, a new curriculum is being constructed from scratch.[14] At many universities, electrical engineering and computer science departments have already merged.

---

[13]"Coming off the Drawing Board: Better Engineers," op. cit., p. 71.

[14]"Schools Nurture Future Leaders," *Florida Today,* p. E2, Jan. 3, 1993.

However, business and financial disciplines have not generally been integrated into technical fields. Despite the fact that engineers and scientists prepare hundreds of reports over the course of their career, their entry-level communications skills are usually high-school level, with little college preparation in technical writing or professional presentations. Basic financial terms, such as the elements of an income statement and balance sheet, are essential for technical leadership yet are mysteries to the young graduate. And most engineering curricula provide no course work in program management techniques, Gantt charts, milestone tracking, or Pareto analysis. Each of these subjects serves as a major performance differentiator among our technical work force, yet they are disregarded in traditional undergraduate (and even graduate) degree programs.

Another serious omission is the absence of a quality focus in our university teaching programs. Coursework on subjects like TQM and statistical process techniques are still few and far between. Who is the customer in the educational process and how are his or her needs met? How often are those needs surveyed? And what is the role of industry, the end user in the educational process?

Despite the obvious need for change, there are several serious barriers that must be overcome to do so:

- The engineering and science curricula are already too intense to allow additional subjects.

- The faculty themselves are isolated from industry needs and are unaware of the seriousness of the deficiencies.

- The accreditation committees for engineering and science programs have a longstanding, inflexible perspective on the number of specific technical courses that are needed for graduation.

The solution to the first barrier is not to add, but to replace. The remedy for the second will be easier as the fac-

TABLE 11.3. Comparison of college preparation for and actual use of selected engineering and communications topics.

Subject	College course preparation	Professional use
Chemical equations	> 2 semesters	Infrequently
Thermodynamic equations	2 semesters	Infrequently
Differential calculus	> 4 semesters	Infrequently
Integral calculus	> 4 semesters	Infrequently
Verbal presentations	Hardly any	Weekly or monthly
Program management techniques	Hardly any	Daily
Written technical reports	Hardly any	Weekly or monthly
Teamwork, collaboration	Hardly any	Daily

ulty become more involved with the new development process and begin to deal with customer participation and customer satisfaction. The third barrier is perhaps the most serious because of the importance for a school to be accredited. But some of the finer schools (departments) are challenging the accreditation committees in the light of outspoken industry needs. Last year, more than a dozen schools threatened to withdraw from the Accreditation Board for Engineering and Technology (ABET) because of its inflexible requirements.[15] An ABET committee is now considering such changes.

The strange imbalance between science and business use is illustrated in Table 11.3. The point here is not to do away with basic science—but to recognize the legitimate place for topics such as communications skills and teamwork in a technical curriculum.

Individual focus

Virtually all engineers in industry work as a member of a team—an employee involvement team, a quality improvement team, a problem-solving team, or a yield enhance-

---

[15]ibid.

ment team. And, as we discussed in chapters 3 through 5, technology and product development are being increasingly carried out by the close daily interactions of empowered work teams. It is probably not an overstatement to say that not more than a handful of individuals in a large corporation work individually for 100 percent of their work-related responsibilities. Despite this cultural theme, the entry-level engineering student comes to the position from a 16-year training program based on individual learning and accomplishment.

In his book on concurrent engineering, Sammy Shina writes:

> "... values of teamwork, the sharing of ideas and goals ... are not taught to engineers in their formal education in U.S. technical colleges and universities, and have to be reinforced by having these characteristics valued just as highly as traditional engineering attributes of technical competency and creativity."[16]

A few obvious techniques come to mind to promote teamwork in the classroom, including the following:

- Team homework, with the same resulting grade for each team member.

- Advanced students tutoring struggling or less experienced teammates.

- Student teams assigned to industry problems.

- National or regional team design competitions.

Such techniques are indeed used from time to time in our universities, but much more as the exception than as the rule.

---

[16]S. G. Shina, op. cit., p. 3.

LOCAL INDUSTRY SUPPORT

U.S. industry is aggressively pursuing all of the topics that constitute the new development paradigm—from concurrent engineering and empowered work teams to TQM and process characterization. But cultural changes are difficult, and the battle has just begun. At this point in the paradigm shift, there are as many questions as answers.

A few universities have jumped aggressively into the fray. Some schools have begun applying TQM to their own organizations; program management techniques are beginning to show up in industrial engineering curricula; and a few universities have begun working on concurrent engineering. But such efforts are still far in the minority.

Opportunities for achieving prominence in this field are almost unlimited. Little capital is needed, since the entire industry structure can serve as the laboratory. A small school with limited expertise can adjust quickly, and move to the forefront—at this moment in time, the new paradigm is sufficiently young to have few established experts.

The following list summarizes areas in which industry needs university support:

- Establishing new courses on product and technology development. Teaching the subject at evening classes and at industry locations.

- Surveying and benchmarking industry status and progress in changing the development process.

- Publishing papers and books based on industry studies to delineate successful versus unsuccessful approaches in adopting the new development paradigm.

- Consulting or advising on techniques to bring about cultural change. Helping establish employee training programs.

- Developing software programs and information systems that extend the CAD approach for product design to the entire development cycle. Recommended actions and timing, archival of key information, and tools such as QFD, Taguchi analysis, and process characterization flow charts should be integral components.

IN SUMMARY

The U.S. university system has been slow to change. In its research and educational programs, universities are based strongly on individual efforts, with only a small dose of teamwork. Its research students are focused on the design and demonstration phases. Customer involvement is limited, and customer support (technology transfer) to industry is difficult. The system's greatest research contribution is educating graduate students, but these students are only trained technically—they lack an understanding of business fundamentals, quality concepts, and the principles of working in teams.

In education, engineering programs are taught today much as they were in 1900—through individual lectures and note-taking. The university student continues to be trained in the style of a rugged individualist—with few lessons on working with others. Finally, the educational curriculum (in science and engineering) is admirably filled with basic courses in these areas, but lacks communications skills, program management, and basic finance. The latter areas are those that differentiate leaders in U.S. businesses.

Opportunities abound for our schools to support the new paradigm in technology and product development. Business needs help in training and educating its employees, and guidance for implementation. But cultural change is essential.

CHAPTER 12

Blueprint
for
Change

Throughout the previous chapters, we discussed the elements of the new development paradigm and its status. In general, most of the elements of this methodology are being pursued aggressively throughout progressive companies within U.S. industry and are at least beginning to gain favor in more conservative companies. But because of the unfamiliar territory being explored, diversions are frequent. In universities, the subject is just beginning to be recognized as important, and efforts in its support are embryonic.

In this final chapter, we outline a blueprint for implementation—first in industry, then in universities. However, keep in mind that the multiple approaches possible require that the blueprint be written in pencil, with revisions almost certainly needed by the reader for any specific organization.

INDUSTRY BLUEPRINT

As we have learned, change is not abnormal. It is the natural consequence of improvement, and it should be embraced. But acceptance of this concept may still be a stretch for much of the U.S. work force. Workers might be willing to accept that change is inevitable, as a consequence of foreign economies catching up to the U.S., but they are probably not ready to admit that it should be sought in its own right as part of the quest for continuous improvement.

There is some good news. By now, most U.S. workers have felt the impact of two decades of the old ways. They've seen plant closings, restructuring, downsizing, and rightsizing; they're lean and mean—or at least smaller in number. And they've heard all about working smarter, not harder. In sum, they've at least survived the lessons of the past and recognize the need to be more competitive and to move more quickly. It isn't too hard to sell a company or a department on the value of rapid new product development. Doing the right things, and doing them right is about as basic as it gets.

And it's already beginning to pay off. U.S. productivity for high-tech corporations is starting to rise. In Figure 12.1, we plot the sales per employee for the 200 largest U.S. elec-

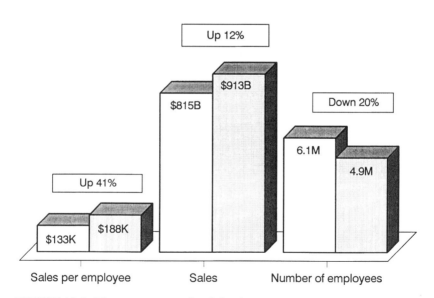

FIGURE 12.1. The average productivity (annual sales per employee) of the largest 200 U.S. electronics companies in 1989 and in 1992.
SOURCE: Data extracted from *Electronic Business*, August 1992, pp. 18–20; July 1993, pp. 44–63.

tronics companies in 1989 and 1992.[1] Over this period, the average sales per employee has increased by 41 percent to $188,000. However, upon closer examination, it turns out that the largest factor in the increase is a 20 percent reduction in the number of employees involved—from 6.1M in 1989 to 4.9M in 1992. And you can bet that a large fraction of this reduction was from middle management through increasing span of control, de-layering, and transferring more responsibilities to the workers and first-line supervisors.

Table 12.1 presents an approximate sequence for implementing the new product and technology development process in a medium-to-large U.S. corporation. For

TABLE 12.1. Major steps for implementation of the new product or technology development paradigm in industry.

1. **Obtain executive buy-in**
    - Management education and training.
    - Mission and vision statement.
    - Resources for new paradigm implementation.
2. **Determine baseline metrics of current development process**
    - Resources used.
    - Development cycle time.
    - New product revenue forecast.
3. **Establish standard development process methodology**
    - Broad participation in defining methodology.
4. **Empower multifunctional development teams**
    - Management and employee training and buy-in.
    - New development metrics.
5. **Select proper products or technology (doing the right products)**
    - Technology roadmaps.
    - Product family roadmaps.
    - QFD for product definition.
6. **Reduce development cycle time (doing the products right)**
    - Distribution and review of key metrics.
    - Pareto charts for bottlenecks and delays.
    - Process characterization.
    - Benchmarking.
7. **Refine the development process**
    - TQM and continuous improvement.

[1]"Electronic Business 200," *Electronic Business*, pp. 18–20, Aug. 1992, "Electronic Business 200," *Electronic Business*, pp. 44–63, July 1993.

completeness, the chart starts in the beginning and assumes that nothing is currently in place. For the practical situation, in which some steps are partially implemented, the adjustments to the chart are straightforward.

Finally, like new product and technology development, the implementation program itself should employ a concurrent approach, include the customers of each particular element, and involve employee teams throughout. The following sections discuss some of the major steps in the sequence.

Executive buy-in

Nothing is as important as obtaining the support and endorsement of the top executive and his or her staff. In fact, without such endorsement, there is little sense in proceeding further. By their actions, the leaders of a company influence the attitude of most other employees. A can-do employee attitude is half the battle. Simply stated, change must be implemented from the bottom up, but it must be initiated and supported from the top down.

Moreover, the changes described throughout this book will require sustained effort over a considerable period of time. Without firm and steady executive support, it will lose momentum and slip back to traditional methods.

Therefore, one of the first responsibilities for implementing the new development methodologies is educating management about the need and the general approach that will be undertaken. Note that we say general approach—since the specifics for any single organization must be determined by the managers and workers themselves.

Baseline metrics

As early as possible, it is important to define a set of metrics and estimate their current values. In this way, a baseline is established against which future progress can be gauged. The definitive, quantitative proof of progress will serve as a strong motivator for continued efforts on the program.

Metrics should be selected with an eye for the future. Although data may well be skimpy at the beginning of the program, metrics similar to some of those discussed in chapter 7 should serve the organization well.

*Standard development
process methodology*

Almost certainly, each organization has a few product development champions who have somehow managed to deal with the existing company departments, personnel, practices, and policies. These folks should lead the effort to document and streamline the development process—making sure that it covers the major elements in each of the five phases. Of course, the process should include front-end planning and definition, and not just the traditional design and demonstration activities. Likewise, it must incorporate marketing and manufacturing activities from the outset.

Once established, the development process should be supported as its methods diffuse throughout the organizations involved. Employee training will speed the implementation and would be especially useful for the initial product or technology teams.

*Empowered multifunctional
development teams*

Since many of these elements will be carried out concurrently, the exact timing and sequence for the use of multifunctional teams is not clear. But a few guidelines may be in order:

- They should follow an overall executive buy-in of the program.

- They should follow the definition of baseline metrics.

It is advisable to initiate just a few teams initially, to identify major problems and to demonstrate early success to other managers and workers. In this way, the use of work teams is pulled by the professional community, rather than pushed by management. In time, employee compensation should be tied to the team's performance, but this should not be done initially.

Proper product or
technology selection

The establishment of technology, manufacturing, and product family roadmaps is a considerable task and must involve teams from each of these organizations. As indicated in chapter 4, the lead should come from the product family requirements, so that is where the effort should initially focus. Remember to involve potential customers throughout the activity.

Cycle time reduction

This is really a set of many activities, which should logically flow from the collection of metric data. Schedule slippage should be reviewed critically for cause, and appropriate methods from chapter 6 should be aggressively applied to the most troublesome.

Development process refinement

The development process should be continually reexamined for ways of making it simpler and more effective. Review the progress that has been made throughout the organization, and especially areas where bottlenecks or problems have been exposed. Be sure the process reflects the most-up-to-date thinking. Expanded training sessions about the process should be held to expand its overall acceptance throughout the organization.

All of the elements in Table 12.1 have been discussed more thoroughly throughout this book. By incorporating these elements in the implementation, and by following the approximate sequence in Table 12.1, an organization can dramatically increase the success of its products in the marketplace.

Finally, it is necessary to set expectations. This program will take many years to implement. Change does not happen overnight—especially when it affects a large fraction of the employee population. Many companies have been at this since the mid-'80s and still have a long way to go. But the benefits are real, and delay is in fact a decision not to compete. As in most worthwhile endeavors, the largest step is the first.

UNIVERSITY BLUEPRINT

Implementation of the new paradigm in a university will be significantly more complex because of the multiple academic missions (education, research, and support) and because of the relative independence that has traditionally been granted to faculty members. However, each university area requires change to keep in step with the overall technology directions that are underway in industry and to a somewhat lesser extent, government.

In Table 12.2, we list the most obvious steps to institute the required changes. The list is not complete—nor is it detailed. As was the case for the industry blueprint, the specific steps can best be established by the academic community itself.

Regarding the research mission, the major challenge is to improve the relevancy of the research. This is best accomplished through strong customer participation and through better planning—both strategic (advanced planning) and tactical (definition). Like it or not, education is a business. Anyone doubting that should check out the tuition fees of $15K to $20K per year in most private universities. And university research must be treated more like a product—it must be driven to a greater extent by market and business needs and to a lesser extent by faculty self interests. University deans and department heads must begin to serve more as leaders and directors of their organization's research activities and less as administrators. The steps indicated in Table 12.2 merely represent some approaches to bringing a more businesslike management attitude to university research. Many academicians will object strenuously to such change—but their customers won't.

In the area of science and engineering education, changes should be instituted in both curricula content and

TABLE 12.2. Suggested steps for implementing the new development paradigm in U.S. universities.

1. **Strategic directions**
   - Establish vision and mission statements for research, teaching, and industry support activities.
2. **Research mission**
   - Establish research roadmaps—meshing targeted university capabilities with future industry needs. Involve industry leaders in roadmap planning.
   - Establish guidelines for pursuing and carrying out university research programs. Demand a realistic proposal that shows relevancy and impact. Strongly encourage collaborative programs with industry.
   - Set up periodic research reviews based not only on technical progress, but on program objectives. Have major customers attend.
   - Establish a procedure for terminating or revising programs that do not meet the original criteria.
   - Set up faculty teams to help each other. In some programs a faculty member would be the leader, in others—the advisor.
   - Establish an active research advisory board comprised of leaders from industry, government, and other research universities.
3. **Teaching mission**
   - Set up a team comprised of faculty and customers (student, parents, and business leaders) to explore ways to enhance curriculum and teaching methodology. Implement (and critically review) student survey of faculty teaching effectiveness.
   - Expand efforts involving student teamwork, communications, financial knowledge, and program management skills.
4. **Industry support mission**
   - Carry out customer surveys (students, industry, government, parents) about desired university support services.
   - Support the new industry development paradigm with courses, seminars, training programs, consulting, and publishing.

teaching methods. The content should be updated to include business subjects that are widely used throughout a professional engineer's career, while the methods should be targeted toward teamwork among students and faculty. Of course, new teaching tools should be encouraged—to more fully exploit the recent advances in electronic communications. Incentives must be given to encourage good teaching practices.

Finally, universities have before them a pressing opportunity to support their industry colleagues in a global struggle for economic survival. There are more questions than answers in the new development paradigm and a great need for educating, training, and consulting. The university community has both the responsibility and the opportunity to make the changes needed to lead the way.

IN SUMMARY

Two charts are presented in chapter 12. The first is a seven-step implementation plan for initiating the new development paradigm in middle-to-large size U.S. corporations. In this chart (Table 12.1), the first and most important step is to obtain a top-level management commitment, for without this, little progress will be made. The second step is to determine the status of the development effectiveness before embarking on a program of change, for a quantitative measure of progress will be necessary to motivate continuation of effort once the initial burst of momentum has faded. The other steps in the implementation plan involve:

- Establishment of a development process methodology.
- Empowerment of work teams.
- Developing technology and product roadmaps.
- Reducing development cycle time.
- Refining the development process.

Each of these subjects has been discussed in detail in earlier chapters.

The second chart in this chapter outlines an approach to enhance the multiple objectives of a university. Here, a focus on relevancy is the central objective of the university research program, while broadening the financial and management skills of the students and teaching them about teamwork are the most important elements of the teaching mission. Finally, Table 13.2 includes a variety of industry support activities that should be embraced by university departments. The university role must be expanded to a position of leadership—not indifference—for the new development paradigm.

Glossary

Activity-Based Cost Accounting An accounting system that categorizes expenses by the product-oriented activities they support, rather than by traditional clumps of expenses. For example product design, qualification testing, and package development, might be used instead of engineering. Activity-based cost accounting is especially helpful in determining the profitability (i.e., income and expense) associated with a particular product or product line.

Advanced planning The first phase of the five-phase development process. In advanced planning, five-year (or more) product-family roadmaps are established and synchronized with long-range technology and manufacturing capabilities.

Applied research The investigation of technologies to determine the means by which a specific, recognized need may be met.

Balance Refers to an appropriate mix of high-risk, new-to-the-world or company-first products versus low-risk product derivatives.

Basic research   The study of phenomena purely for the purpose of gaining more complete knowledge or understanding of the subject under study, without specific applications in mind.

Benchmarking   Rating a company's practices, processes, or products against the world's best, including those in other industries.

Break-even time   The time between when a product begins development and when its cumulative sales revenue equals the cumulative development cost.

Company first   A product or technology being developed which is unlike others from that company. At least one other company is known to have such a capability, otherwise the product or technology would be labeled new to the world.

Complacency   An attitude prevalent in the United States between approximately 1950 and 1975, in which our industrial and technology superiority was generally assumed to be invulnerable. This led to complacency in our work force in terms of entitlements to benefits that were often not merited.

Concurrent   Occurring at the same time. Happening simultaneously.

Concurrent engineering/concurrent development   A parallel development approach for reducing time to market, as well as for improving the quality and market impact of new products. Concurrent teams are comprised of representatives from engineering, manufacturing, marketing, and quality, who attempt to carry out as much of the development process as possible in parallel. The team makes special efforts to anticipate problems and issues that might occur throughout the development process and resolve them in advance.

Consortium A group of organizations formed to undertake a common objective that is beyond the resources or capabilities of any single member organization. Plural: consortia.

Continuous improvement Searching unceasingly for ever-higher levels of quality by isolating sources of defects or problems—and eliminating them.

Core competencies The few longstanding technical or product capabilities or business practices that distinguish a specific company from its competitors.

Customer A user of the products or technology being developed. A customer can be external (e.g., another company) or internal (e.g., another department in the same organization). In either case, customer satisfaction is the key to successful development.

Customer support The final phase of the development process, during which the normal sales and manufacturing organizations assume primary responsibility for the product. The essential element in this phase is the desire and availability of the development team to assist in any way possible to make the transition successful.

Definition The second phase of the five-phase development process. The key activities in this phase are linking product features to customer requirements, and preparing a detailed business plan for the proposed product. By the end of the definition phase, the organization must be convinced that the proposed product is the right product, and that the proposed plan develops the product in the right fashion.

Demonstration   The fourth phase of the five-phase development process, in which product or technology prototypes are prepared and evaluated over a wide range of conditions (such as operating temperature and manufacturing variables). The demonstration phase includes qualifying the product or technology for customer use.

Derivative   A product or technology that is derived from an existing basic capability. Product derivatives are usually relatively straightforward to develop because of the prior experience and existing capability. Also called extension.

Design   The third phase of the five-phase development process, in which all of the technical elements of the product or technology design are specified. The design should comprehend and minimize manufacturing and test variations (DFM and DFT).

Design for manufacturing (DFM)   A method that uses statistical characterization of the manufacturing process to ensure that the product design falls within the parameters of normal manufacturing variances for each process element. This allows the designer to optimize the design for performance and manufacturing yield.

Design for test (DFT)   A design methodology that produces designs for which tests can be generated by known methods. Such methods reduce test generation and testing costs, while providing higher-quality products.

Design Reuse   The process by which a specific subset of software (module) can be isolated, then archived for subsequent incorporation into other programs.

Design review/design release   A formal review that is carried out at the completion of the design phase. The detailed design plan, including all technical, manufacturing, and marketing plans are reviewed by management as an important gate before the product continues to demonstration or prototyping. The product is said to be released when it is approved for continued development.

Development (1) The systematic application of advanced knowledge or technology toward the production of useful materials, devices, systems, or methods; (2) The comprehensive, five-step process for completing the planning, definition, design, demonstration, and customer support (satisfaction) associated with a new product or technology.

Empowerment The act of providing authority and responsibility to a work team for the purpose of carrying out the day-to-day development of a specific product or technology. To be effective, such empowerment also must be supported with sufficient resources for the team to complete their objective.

Enabling technology A technology capability that is used by or incorporated into products that are undergoing development. Typical examples are a design system or a specific manufacturing process.

Fabrication The front-end part of the manufacturing process for making products. It is contrasted to assembly—the back-end part of the manufacturing process.

Facilitator A person who supports and assists the actions of a work team. Managers responsible for self-directed work teams must spend a considerable portion of their time facilitating the efforts of their teams. Facilitators should possess motivational and coaching abilities.

First of a kind A product or technology that has not been previously developed by any other known organization. Such products often are considered high risk but usually provide high payback, if successful.

Gain sharing   The practice by which some or all of a work team's compensation (salary) is determined directly by the successful completion of agreed-upon team milestones and objectives. The metrics for such a program must be very carefully established and communicated before the start of the program.

Gantt chart   A program scheduling chart that shows the forecast and actual timing of key program milestones, as well as their sequence. The chart is commonly used to review a program's progress versus its plan.

House of quality   A conceptual technique, first developed in Japan, for examining the multiple interactions between product requirements and engineering capabilities. The four axes used in the graphical implementation of this concept produce a profile similar to the sketch of a house, hence its name.

Individualism   The emphasis on individual accomplishment, in contrast to team-oriented performance. Such behavior is fostered in the United States by an individual-based culture and is reinforced by our education system.

Intellectual property   Patents, copyrights, and trade marks; these protect the product and its concepts from use by other companies, without first negotiating fees and conditions for their use.

Keiretsu   A single Japanese cooperative organization consisting of a large number of corporations in such fields as finance, electronics, materials, transportation, chemicals, and metals. The mission of the Keiretsu is to assist its membership through preferential purchasing policies with each other and through targeted business objectives in strategically important industries. The companies in Japan's six largest keiretsus constitute 78 percent of the value of the Tokyo Stock Exchange.

Market pull   When the characteristics of a new product are being driven by customer or market requirements, rather than by the capabilities of the existing technology. See also *Technology push.*

Metric   An agreed-upon measure for determining the relative or absolute progress of a development team (or a group of teams) toward its specific objective.

Multifunctional   Pertains to a work team whose members have several different functional capabilities—such as design, manufacturing, quality, marketing, and sales. Such a team is capable of resolving a wide variety of problems without outside help.

Net present value (NPV)   The current financial value of future cash flow. NPV takes into account the fact that future revenue must be discounted by the interest that would accrue on that investment over time.

Paradigm   A pattern or approach that is considered by knowledgeable people to be the right way of doing something. In the product or technology development process, a paradigm shift is required to change the isolated, sequential, individual-based methodology to that led by empowered self-directed work teams.

Pareto chart   A bar graph that rank orders the causes of process variation by their overall impact.

Process characterization   A technique by which an organization, with the help of a facilitator, examines its internal procedures with the objective to streamline the process. A commonly used tool for this purpose is a flow chart that highlights the sequence of events as well as the bottleneck areas.

Product development   The five-phase process by which a product passes from conception to market introduction and volume production.

Product   That which is produced, manufactured, grown, written, or otherwise created. The result of any serious work effort.

Product family   A group (family) of products that are closely related in functionality and which evolve from a single product capability.

Product roadmap   A chart that shows the timing of product introductions (over a period of several years) for the members of a product family.

Prototype   The initial version of a product that is prepared to explore its feasibility and potential operating characteristics.

Product-to-market time   The time required to develop a new product, usually measured from initiation of the development process to market introduction.

Quality function deployment (QFD)   A planning and analysis methodology used to ensure that customer requirements are optimally coupled with product design solutions.

Reengineering   A method by which a fresh evaluation is made of organizational procedures or culture with little concern for their evolutionary basis. A "clean sheet of paper" approach to organizational methods that seeks nontraditional breakthrough results.

Return factor A metric for calculating the financial return for a specific product investment. The ratio of the total operating profit (over the life of a product) to the total product development cost.

Reuse See *Design reuse.*

Right product Refers to the selection of a product to undergo development that is strategically aligned with the company's core competencies, is in synchronization with the company's enabling technology and manufacturing roadmaps, and has been meshed with major customers' requirements. Such a product is much more likely to achieve market success and profitability than another that has not undergone such planning.

Robust design A design practice that seeks to reduce the product sensitivity to the sources of variability through careful selection of design rules.

Quality function deployment (QFD) A methodology for developing products that meet the needs of the customer. A graphic technique for comparing customer benefits and requirements against engineering capabilities and interdependencies. See *House of quality.*

Self-directed work team A work team that has been empowered by management to complete a specific program. In product and technology development, such a team is usually multifunctional (containing team members from design, manufacturing, marketing, and quality) and attempts to carry out as many of its tasks as possible concurrently.

Sematech (**SE**miconductor **MA**nufacturing **TECH**nology Research Consortium). A consortium of 14 U.S. semiconductor manufacturing firms dedicated to restoring America's leadership in semiconductor manufacturing. It was founded in 1987 and is located in Austin, Texas.

Semiconductor Research Corporation   A consortium of approximately 60 member companies and government agencies that plan and execute programs of semiconductor research at leading U.S. universities to strengthen the long-term competitive stability of the semiconductor industry. It was founded in 1982, and is located in Research Triangle Park, North Carolina.

Statistical process control (SPC)   A statistical analysis technique to ensure that a manufacturing process is controlled to the limits of its capability. Rather than finding defects through direct inspection, SPC attempts to monitor drifts in the process itself.

Supplier   The source of the material or information input to a manufacturing process. Suppliers can be internal or external to an organization.

Taguchi methods   A set of statistical techniques developed by Genichi Taguchi for optimizing product design.

Target market   The market segment that has been selected for product launch based on product features versus customer market requirements. A product can have more than one target market.

Taylorism   Refers to the business management philosophy espoused by Frederick Taylor (1856–1915), an efficiency expert who developed the leading theory of manufacturing management throughout the first half of the 20th century. Taylor's concepts refer to a division between managers as thinkers and all other employees as doers.

Technology push   The occurrence whereby the characteristics of a new product are being driven by the capabilities of the existing technology, rather than by the needs of the customer or market. See also *Market pull*.

Technology roadmap A description of the strategic (5-year plus) plan for research and development in an enabling technology area, such as wafer processing, design systems, packaging, and test systems. Roadmaps are usually comprised of a simplified graphic description of the plan, supplemented with documents that contain the descriptive details.

Total quality management (TQM) The application of quality principles to all company endeavors, including satisfying both internal and external customers as well as seeking to make tomorrow's efforts always more effective than today's. Sometimes referred to as total quality control (TQC).

Virtual integration The formation of a supplier chain that provides all elements of the final customer solution. Virtual integration refers to the fact that the chain is comprised of different companies whose plans and commitments are tightly meshed—just as if they were a single organization.

Vision statement The guiding statement that contains the ideals and long-term goals of a company or an organization.

Index